the best of

PRAGUE

PRA HA
PRA GUE
PRA GA
PRA G

St. Vitus Cathedral – wall painting in St. Wenceslas Chapel

the best of
PRAGUE

Publisher: Vydavatelství MCU s. r. o.
Hany Kvapilové 10, 370 10 České Budějovice,
Tel./Fax: +420/387 428 360, E-mail: info@mcumedia.cz; www.mcumedia.cz
Technical editors: Radek Eliášek, Petr Steinbauer
Text: Viktor Kubík, Pavel Dvořák
Translation: Stewart Aitchison, Carolyn Zukowski
Foto: Libor Sváček; Fotobanka.cz (7); ČTK (1)
Typesetting: Vydavatelství MCU, Pavel Dvořák (responsible editor)
Maps, plans: SHOCart Zlín; Atp, Tomáš Rygl
Print: Typodesign České Budějovice, s. r. o.
Distribution: MCU Praha, Poděbradská 540/26, 190 00 Praha 9 – Vysočany, tel.: +420/225 277 350,
e-mail: mcu.praha@velkoobchodmcu.cz

2nd Edition, České Budějovice, 2009
16th publication, 144 pages

ISBN 80-7339-068-X (angl. vyd.)

TABLE OF CONTENTS

(page 76)

Pražská informační služba

YOUR PARTNER IN PRAGUE

www.prague-info.cz

PRAGA CAPUT REI PUBLICAE

Prague, the capital city of the Czech Republic, extends along the Vltava River, in the middle of the Czech Basin. Czech Republic's biggest city, Prague covers over 500 square kilometres and houses 12 % of its population. Prague's beautifully preserved historic core earned it a place on the UNESCO list in 1992.

The earliest settlements date from the 4th millennium B.C. The most important **prehistoric** finds come from Šárka or Únětice, near present-day Prague. At that time, it was the most significant settlement in the Czech Basin. This area was also a very substantial part of the **Celtic** world during the Hallstatt period in the 6th century B.C. Around 1 A.D., the **Germanic tribes** arrived. They took over this region from the Celtic Boii tribe, later calling it *Boiohaemum*, "the home of the Boii" now Bohemia. Bohemia then became their home for the next five hundred years. The **Slavs** replaced them at the turn of the 5th and 6th centuries and it is with them that the creation of Prague in its present position is first associated. The increasing requirements of the state led to the creation of Prague Castle, which served as the residence of

Hradčany Square   Prague Castle   St. Vitus Cathedral   Lobkovicz Palace

Panorama of the Castle and Malá Strana (the Lesser Town) from Petřín

Bohemian princes from as early as the 9th century.

The Přemyslid Empire and Přemyslid Prague grew with the spread of Christianity, which Saints Cyril and Methodius brought to the people in the Slavic language in 863. Prague was already an imposing city in the 10th century, as Jewish traveller Ibrahim Ibn Jakob described it as a rich "stone town." The rise of the capital city reflected the prosperity of the Czech Lands. After more than five hundred years on the throne, the Přemyslids not only ruled Bohemia, Moravia and Silesia from Prague but they had also obtained the Polish and Hungarian Kingdoms. The riches of the Kutná Hora silver mines inspired frenzy comparable to the 19th century Klondike gold rush, and silver Prague *groschen* represented one of the most stable currencies in Europe for the following three centuries. Unfortunately, the state immediately disintegrated when young Wenceslas III, the last of the Přemyslids, was murdered in Olomouc in 1306. The city of Prague remained a shining example of power and beauty for central Europe, which the Luxembourgs and Jagiellonians emulated. Later, the Habsburgs restored and united central Europe.

| Schönborn Palace | St. Nicholas Church | Church of the Victorious Virgin Mary | Charles Bridge |

The head of Héro the Celt

The Luxembourgs ruled for nearly one hundred and thirty years (1310–1437). Wenceslas, son of John of Luxembourg, and raised in the Paris court, took the name of Charles as their most distinguished representative. He obtained the imperial crown and was from then on known as **Charles IV.** Prague, the capital city of Bohemia and the Holy Roman Empire, transformed itself into a city unlike any other in Europe at that time. Charles' son, Wenceslas IV, was unable to follow his successful father's example during difficult times. The old world collapsed, Bohemian fine arts boomed, and the stage for the first Reformation was set in Prague.

The Czech Reformation happened one hundred years earlier than the European Reformation. The Czech Lands paid a cruel price for this, with numerous civil wars, a plethora of crusades and forbidding papal laws, which plagued the Bohemian countryside for most of the 15th century. Not even the capable Hussite King George of Poděbrady was

able to turn around this unfavourable development. A golden age had ended.

The rulers of the **Jagiellonian Dynasty**, who wanted to lead the country out of crisis, had a lot of great ambitions, but unfortunately lesser abilities. The tragic death of King Louis in the Battle of Mohács (1526) ended the more than fifty year reign of the Jagiellonians, and opened the way for the Turks to invade Hungary and for the Habsburgs to gain power.

The Habsburgs held together the states of Austria, Bohemia and Hungary for almost four hundred years until 1918. The age of the Renaissance accompanied them in their accession to the Czech throne, and a newly Protestant

Prague groschen (1st half of the 14th century)

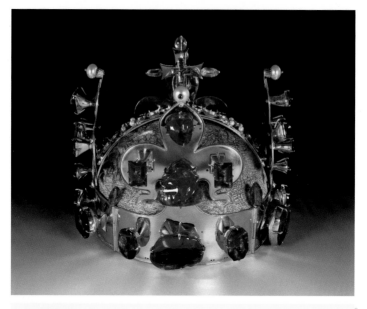

St. Wenceslas' Crown
Charles IV had the symbol of Czech statehood made for his coronation as King of Bohemia in 1347. The crown, kept in St.Vitus Cathedral in Prague Castle, is made of pure gold, and is richly decorated with sapphires, rubies, and emeralds.

environment emerged. Emperor Rudolf II moved his residence to Prague in 1584, and it seemed the city would recover its glory. Rudolf II's Prague became a centre of Mannerism in Europe, artfully pursuing the representation of idealized beauty.

After the death of Rudolph II, the conflict of the Protestant majority with the Catholic Habsburgs ended in the rebellion of the estates, which ushered in the **Thirty Years' War** (1618–1648). The Czech Protestants lost, and the Czech lands became a provincial backwater as most of the Czech nobles, intelligentsia and patricians emigrated. A period of cruel re-Catholicization took place. The rampaging wars murdered half of the population of the Czech Lands and the

troops plundered the Royal Bohemian and Rudolphine collections. Even so, during the war the ambitious imperial general Albrecht of Wallenstein tried to maintain the Rudolph II's artistic tradition. His imposing palace in the Lesser Town (Malá Strana) thus ushered in the monumental buildings of Prague's **Baroque Period.** Prague changed its appearance again. The cooperation of talented artists and generous patrons runs from the last half of the 17th and to the first part of the18th century.

The Enlightenment of the 18th century brought the decline of artistic vigour and a lapse into provincialism. The enforcement of German as the official state language coupled with the cultural barbarity of the Josephine reforms

devastated the country and threatened the survival of the Czech language. The **National Revival** movement swiftly followed, as a response to this "century of Enlightenment". It did not only involve the Czech nation, but also the German-speaking minority. The tragic manner of defining a nation by language laid the foundations for the national rift between the Czech-and German-speaking Czechs. Paradoxically, at this time, excellent Czech literature written in German was published, climaxing at the turn of the 19th and 20th centuries with authors such as Franz Kafka, Gustav Meyrink (Meyer), and Franz Werfel.

The works of the 19th century, including Prague Art Nouveau, complemented the Baroque character of Medieval Prague, but did not change its character. In the end, not even the **modern movements** of the beginning of the 20th century damaged the appearance of old Prague. An example of this can be found in Prague's unique pre-World War I Cubist architecture.

World War I swept away the Habsburg Monarchy. On October 28th, 1918, the formation of the **Czechoslovak Republic** was proclaimed, Prague became a thriving capital city, and Prague Castle welcomed the first President of the Czechoslovak Republic, Thomas Garrigue Masaryk. In the late 1920's, Art Nouveau was replaced by Functionalism and Surrealism. The twenty-year period of the First Republic was the second golden age in the country's history, terminated by the Munich Agreement in 1938, when Britain and France delivered the country to Hitler. The **occupation** by fascist Germany once again threatened the existence of the Czech-speaking majority. The atrocities that the Nazis committed made relations between Czechs and Czech Germans – 98 % of whom later chose to be German Germans – impossible. The Prague Uprising in May 1945 heralded the return of freedom. The post-war **expulsion** of 2.5 million Germans from the Czech lands ended 700 years of cohabitation between Czech and German-speakers. After the Munich experience with the western allies and impressed by the liberation of most of the Czech lands by Russia, many Czechs believed it would be possible to combine democracy with communism. 40 % of the votes sufficed for the communists to mount a coup d'etat in 1948.

With creative enthusiasm, the **Communist Dictatorship** attempted to destroy everything that was reminiscent of a bygone era. Fortunately, the communists did not have as much strength as they would have wished.

Charles IV of Luxembourg
The Holy Roman Emperor and Bohemian King lived from 1316 to 1378. In the Czech Lands he has been known since his death as "Father of Bohemia" His exceptional abilities as a statesman, and skill at marrying into noble families enabled him to expand the borders of Bohemia. Prague was the centre of his empire and one of the richest and most advanced cities in Europe. He founded significant institutions here such as Charles University, The New Town (Nové Město), St. Vitus Cathedral, Charles Bridge, Karlštejn Castle, and many churches, monasteries, and castles. You can see his likeness in the sculptural group from E. J. Hähnel (1848) near the Old Town Bridge Tower.

Ball Game Pavilion

St. Vitus's Cathedral

Hradčanské Square

PRAGUE CASTLE

Prague and its castle are inextricably linked. The significance of Prague Castle as a political and religious centre has not actually changed at all from its most ancient origins and has been the most sacred centre of Bohemia for 1,200 years. Prague Castle's vantage point above the Vltava was advantageous for protection, and a settlement started on the banks of the Vltava. Archaeological evidence shows that a market grew up on the site of the present-day Lesser Town from the 8th century. A settlement developed on Hradčany during this period and it is highly probable that the religious and political function of Prague Castle arose at this time.

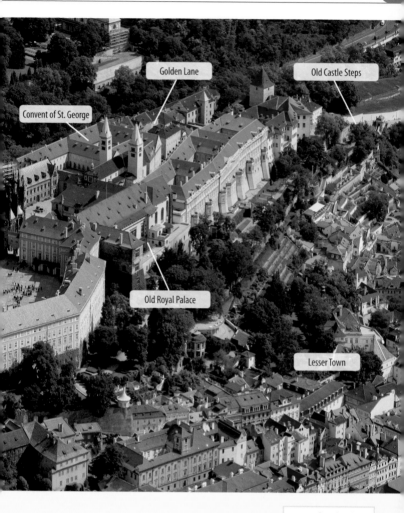

Golden Lane

Old Castle Steps

Convent of St. George

Old Royal Palace

Lesser Town

www.hrad.cz/en

The oldest written records about the complex date from 880. At that time the Přemyslid Prince **Bořivoj** had it fortified and transferred his residence here from Levý Hradec, where he had built a palace earlier, and founded the Church of the Virgin Mary which is the second oldest in the Czech Republic. Archaeologists have established that **the Prague Castle heights were the religious and political centre of Bohemia by 850 A.D.** Bohemian nobles assembled, chose their Princes, and put them on the throne. At the same time, they worshiped the old pagan pre-Christian gods.

Entrance to the Castle through the Gate of the Giants, with Matyáš Gate in the background ❶

irreconcilable differences mounted between the Czechs and Slovaks, about how to run the state mounted between the Slovaks and the Czechs. Since 1993, Prague has been the capital city of the Czech Republic, which on March 12th, 1999 entered **NATO** and on the May 1st, 2004 the **European Union.**

After the tanks from "friendly" soviet block countries crushed an attempt at "socialism with a human face", the era of normalization arrived, in which devastation of Czech cultural heritage progressed more systematically.

On November 17th, 1989, **The Velvet Revolution** enabled Czechs to return to a self-determining state. Prague once again woke up to freedom. Free elections meant the division of Czechoslovakia, also known as **The Velvet Divorce**, as

PRAGUE CASTLE
THE NEW PALACE,
FIRST AND SECOND COURTYARDS

Nowadays, Prague Castle's **New Palace** is the administrative seat of the President of the Czech Republic. The Viennese court architect, Nicola Pacassi, built its wings in the late 18th century to unify the individual castle palaces, particularly those from the time of Rudolf II.

The main entrance to Prague Castle was always on the western side facing Hradčanské náměstí (Hradčany

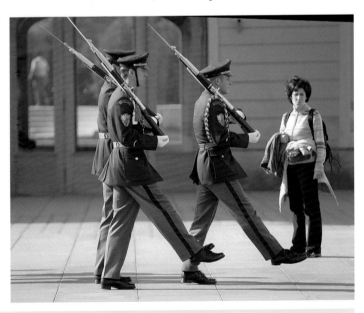

The Changing of the Guard at the First Courtyard of Prague Castle

2nd Courtyard – the Chapel of the Holy Cross and the Renaissance Well and Baroque Kohl Fountain

Square). At one time, there was a ravine separating the spur of Prague Castle from the adjoining Hradčany on the site of the present-day First Courtyard. During the 10th century, the ravine was transformed into a deep moat, and in the 14th century, two more moats were added. Nicola Pacassi changed the thousand-year entrance to the castle by filling in the ditches and creating the area of the First Courtyard. It is actually an honorary courtyard, dominated by the **Gate of the Giants** [1] with sculptural decoration and the Late Manneristic **Matyáš Gate** from 1614, which continues into the western wing of the **New Palace.** Its architectural appearance demonstrates what the corresponding Rudolphine buildings could have looked at Prague Castle.

The entrance hallway of the Matyáš Gate divides the west wing: the southern part boasts Rococo decorated interiors from the 18th century and the monumental Column Hall of Josip Plečnik, constructed in the early 1920s, dominates the northern part. Its original, yet traditionally respectful style enchanted the President T. G. Masaryk.

The northern part of the west wing continues up to the most impressive space of the presidential part of Prague Castle – the **Spanish Hall.** Rudolph II commissioned its construction in 1602 for court celebrations.

Built at the same time as the north wing, where there had been stables from the beginning of the 16th century, the Prague Castle Picture Gallery cannot compete with its previous Rudolphine

Third Courtyard of Prague Castle ❸

riches. Nevertheless, the collection here is a worthy successor with works by Lucas Cranach the Elder, Hans von Aachen, Tizian, and Peter Paul Rubens. The area of the Second Courtyard is dominated by the Baroque **Fountain**

The windows of Vladislav Hall have a Renaissance character ❹

built in 1686, a Renaissance well with a decorative cover from the 18th century and the **Chapel of the Holy Cross [2]** built in the mid-18th century. The period fittings of its interior were installed during the 19th century.

The Palace Wings around the Second Courtyard now serve as representative and presidential offices. The Rococo and Classicist interiors were linked by the tasteful adaptations of Josip Plečnik, T. G. Masaryk's architect in the 1920s. He was responsible for the **Impluvium** as the central space of the presidential flat at the division of the south and west wings, the **Harp Stateroom**, but also the **Lift** and other spaces).

Tradition at Prague Castle goes hand in hand with a vibrant present. In the 1990s, contemporary art chosen by Václav Havel's architect, Bořek Šípek enlivened the New Palace wing on the Second Courtyard.

Vladislav Hall ⑤

THE THIRD COURTYARD AND THE OLD ROYAL PALACE

Part of the courtyard south of the cathedral is decorated by a **monolith of black granite** [3], erected in 1928 as a memorial to the victims of the First World War. There is also a replica of the **bronze group of statues of St George** (the original dating from 1373 is now in the National Gallery) and the **Old Provost's Office** [3], which is located at the Palace of the Prague Bishops. The original appearance of this palace has been preserved on the surface of the facade from which part of the stonework and an associated Romanesque window from 1142 protrude. The original group of statues of St. George is the oldest preserved bronze equestrian statue in central Europe.

Under the **Old Royal Palace** we come across **Romanesque halls** dating from 1135, when Prince Soběslav had his breathtakingly beautiful seat built here "in the manner of a Roman town", as a contemporary chronicler recorded. A barrel vault spans the preserved cellar halls and it is possible to see the uncovered remains of a much older rampart fortification, perhaps dating from the 10th century. Originally, these rooms

The so-called Vladislav's Bedroom ⑥

Riding Staircase

served as food stores, wine cellars and occasionally, as a prison or dungeon.

The **Gothic ground floor** from the Luxemburg period is above the

Romanesque cellars. It dates from the time of Charles IV (1333). Arcades, which Wenceslas IV had partially walled up (around 1400), opened onto the courtyard. A series of halls is located behind them – the most notable is the **Column Hall of Wenceslas IV** (around 1400). Its Late Gothic-styled living area is one of the most luxurious in the palace.

The **Late Gothic and Renaissance floor** [4] is located above the Luxembourg Gothic ground floor. It mainly dates from the Jagiellonian period (1471–1526) and mainly served for courtly purposes from the earliest times. The outer windows and inner portals illustrate the first echoes of the Italian Renaissance in Bohemia.

The Late Gothic **Vladislav Throne Room** [5] dominates the whole floor. Architect Benedict Ried, replaced the

Rooms for the New Country Panels

original halls of the Luxembourg Palace between 1486 and 1502, creating the largest vaulted space without internal buttressing in the European world. This was the venue for coronation celebrations, representational banquets and ceremonies. Here you would find important parliaments assembled, tournaments taking place and luxury goods sold as well. Today, this is the venue for announcing newly elected Presidents of the Czech Republic and other significant political ceremonies.

The seat of the Bohemian Court Office was located in the Renaissance-styled **Ludwig's Wing** [8] in 1509, named after Ludwig Jagiellon. Czech Protestants threw the Catholic vice regents of the estates out of the window of the second room of the Bohemian Court Office on May 23rd, 1618. This protest against the erosion of provincial freedom and the limiting of religious tolerance marked the beginning of the Rising of the Estates and the resultant Thirty Years' War.

Old Parliament

Late-Gothic **Vladislav's Bedroom** [6] is located in the wing above Wenceslas' Columned Hall. It is, in reality, a small audience hall, with rich stone and painted ornamentations dating from the late 15th century.

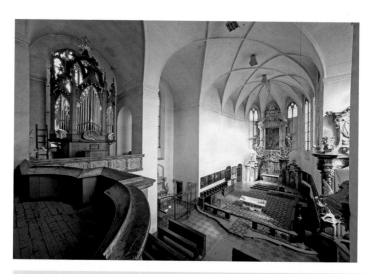

Old Royal Palace – The Church of All Saints

Ludwig´s Wing 8

The Renaissance wing of the Royal Palace was entered in the history books on the 23rd of May, 1618, as Protestant aristocrats threw some royal vice regents out of the window. Although all of them survived, the act of protest provoked the unleashing of the rising of the estates, which started the Thirty Years' War in Europe. This was already the Third Defenestration of Prague: The first, in 1419, led to the occupation of Prague by the Hussites and subsequently to the Hussite Revolution; the second, in 1483, took place during the uprising of the Protestants against the Catholics.

The **Church of All Saints** [7] adjoins the Royal Palace from the eastern side. Its original, 12th century Romanesque appearance made way for Gothic renovations, commissioned by Charles IV. In the late 14th century, architect Petr Parléř finished the church, which was destroyed by fire in 1541. In 1580, the church was restored, extended and directly connected to Vladislav Hall. In 1588, the remains of St. Prokop, Bohemian patron saint were placed here. He was the founder of Sázava Monastery, where the Great Moravian Old Slav Liturgy was kept until the end of the

11th century. The present-day fittings of the church are mainly Baroque, but the side altar triptych of the Holy Angels from the end of the 16th century is the work of an excellent painter from the Rudolphine Court – perhaps by Hans von Aachen himself.

ST. VITUS CATHEDRAL

The true heart of the Czech state and the most sacred place for all Czechs is situated in the middle of the main Third Courtyard. In earlier times, the Rotunda of St. Vitus founded by St. Wenceslas in 925, was located here on the present day site of **St. Vitus Cathedral** [9]. In the 11th century, the Chapel of St. Wenceslas succeeded the Romanesque Basilica that once stood here. It served as a Cathedral to the Prague Archbishops, as well as a coronation and burial place for Bohemian rulers.

The body of St. Wenceslas, eternal king and protector of Bohemia reposes in the **Chapel of St. Wenceslas** [12] and the **Crown Jewels** [13] are deposited above the chapel in the Coronation Chamber. St. Wenceslas Chapel, built under Charles IV by Petr Parléř (1367) demonstrates the significance of this place. Its square ground plan actually disrupts the usual scheme of a cathedral ground plan of the day, because it was not possible to relocate the holy grave of the main patron of the country. It was the wish of Charles IV to demonstrate this. Covered with bright semi-precious stones and frescoes, the walls of St. Wenceslas Chapel dating from the 16th century recount the legend of St. Wenceslas. The two-metre stone **Statue**

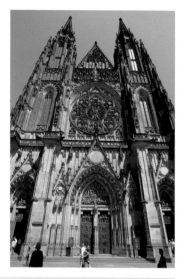

Western Neo-Gothic facade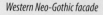

Spiral staircase

of St. Wenceslas (1373) and frescoes depicting the Passion and the portraits of Charles IV and his fourth wife, Eliška Pomořanská date from the time of Charles IV. The completely exceptional star vault of the chapel also dates to the reign of Charles IV. The other fittings are Renaissance, except for the Neo-

Main nave of St. Vitus Cathedral

**Crown Jewels
of the Bohemian Kings**

The Czech Crown Jewels are stored in the Royal Chamber of St. Vitus Cathedral behind a door with seven locks. In this way, under the additional symbolic protection of St. Wenceslas, the patron saint of the country, the most valuable Czech treasure – the Coronation Insignia of the Bohemian Kings – is protected.

The crown was first used in 1347 (more on page 7). The apple and sceptre come from a later period, probably from the 1st half of the 16th century, made from very fine gold, sapphires and pearls.

Gothic gilded chandelier and the altar tombstone of St. Wenceslas dating from 1913.

A dominant feature of the southern façade is the **Great Southern Tower** capped with a Renaissance gallery and a Baroque onion cupola. The core is, however, by Petr Parléř as is the adjacent **spiral staircase [10]**, a technical marvel of its era. Its axis changes direction in three places and the whole construction evokes an unusually lightweight effect as the outer casing consists of a decorative network of ribs. Its creator was probably Petr Parléř or his sons. A Renaissance clock from the end of the 16th century

St. Wenceslas Chapel

was added to the Great Tower as was a gilt window grate. Rudolph II donated this latter feature and the biggest bell is behind it – the sixteen ton, Zikmund (1549).

The **Golden Gate** forms the monumental entrance to the cathedral between the Great Southern Tower and the St. Wenceslas Chapel. Its vaulted entrance hall was constructed in an unbelievably complicated manner by using "free rib

12

technique", where free space is lined with structural buttresses. Although it is a work of the 1360s, it anticipated practices which were in use about one hundred years later. The outer frontal wall of the Golden Gate is decorated with a **mosaic** [15] from the time of Charles IV on which he is portrayed with his fourth wife, Eliška Pomořanská. Venetian mosaic makers made it in 1371 according to designs by Czech painters. It is the biggest and oldest outdoor mosaic north of the Alps.

Petr Parléř's workshop not only made the Chapel of St. Wenceslas and the Golden Gate with the South Tower, but also the presbytery of the cathedral up to the **Old Sacristy**, roofed with a bold vault with a suspended apex stone. Built in 1356, this was a technically superlative performance in its day. **The Vault of the Presbytery** built in 1385 by Petr

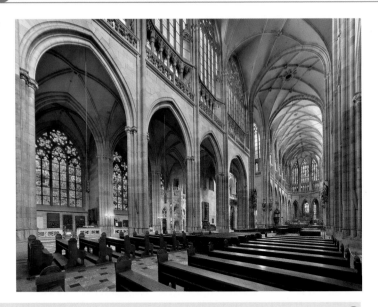

St. Vitus' Cathedral – view in the direction of the main altar **11**

Parléř, is one of the oldest net vaults in Europe. Late Gothic architectural designs produced during construction of the Prague cathedral were replicated almost a century later throughout central Europe.

The busts of the lower triforium are rare not only in regards to their

Window panes by M. Švabinský **14**

realistic design, but in their subject matter. Members of noble houses and the highest church dignitaries in the kingdom are depicted as well as both of the cathedral architects (Matyáš of Arras and Petr Parléř) and five building directors. Paying tribute to the artists themselves was quite unusual in the Middle Ages and demonstrates the pre-Renaissance character of the Prague Court of Charles IV.

Some of the original painted decorations have also been preserved in the individual chapels of the presbytery – **Gothic wall paintings** from the end of the 14th century.

The remains of older buildings have been preserved **under the cathedral,** where you'll find the eastern **Crypts of St. Cosmas and Damion** from the 11th century, the southern masonry and northern apses of the **St. Vitus Rotunda**, as well as tombs for the Kings of Bohemia and their wives.

ST. VITUS CATHEDRAL

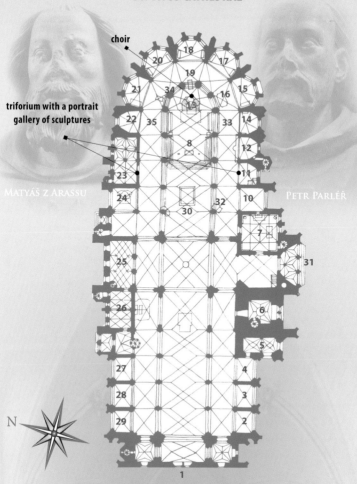

choir

triforium with a portrait gallery of sculptures

MATYÁŠ Z ARRASU

PETR PARLÉŘ

N

1. main entrance (west facade)
2. Chapel of St. Ludmilla
3. Chapel of the Lord´s Tomb
4. Thun Chapel
5. Capitular Library
6. Hasenburg Chapel
   entrance to the tower gallery
7. Chapel of St. Wenceslas
   (Coronation Cabinet)
8. Royal Mausoleum
9. Pulpit
10. Chapel of St. Andrew (Martinická)
11. Chap. of the Holy Cross, entrance to the Royal Crypts
12. Royal oratory
13. Main altar
14. Chapel of St. Mary Magdalene (Vladštejnská)
16. Tombstone of St. John Nepomuk
17. Chapel of the Holy Relics (Saská or Šternberská)
18. Chapel of Mother Mary (Císařská)

19. Altar of St. Vitus
20. Chapel of St. John the Baptist
21. The Archbishop´s Chapel (Pernštejnská)
22. Chapel of St. Anne (Nostická)
23. The Old Sacristy, former Chap. of St. Michael
24. Chapel of St. Sigmund (Černínská)
25. Choir Chapel
26. The New Sacristy
27. The New Archbishop´s Chapel
28. The Schwarzenberg Chapel
29. Chapel of the Bartoňs of Dobenín
30. Exit from the crypts
31. The Golden Gate (southern facade)
32. Monument to Field Marshal Count
    Leopold Šlik
33. Two-part carved picture of the
    devastated Cathedral of St. Vitus
34. Bronze statue of the kneeling
    Cardinal Bedřich Schwarzenberk

www.hrad.cz/en

PRAGUE CASTLE

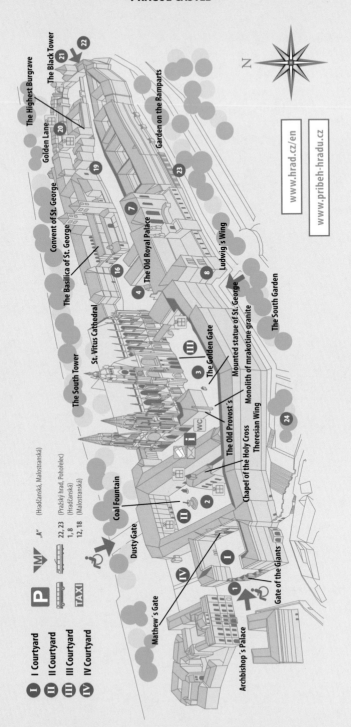

www.hrad.cz/en

www.pribeh-hradu.cz

- **I** I Courtyard
- **II** II Courtyard
- **III** III Courtyard
- **IV** IV Courtyard

P
M „A" (Hradčanská, Malostranská)
22, 23 (Pražský hrad, Pohořelec)
1, 8 (Hradčanská)
12, 18 (Malostranská)
TAXI

The Black Tower
The Highest Burgrave
Golden Lane
Convent of St. George
The Basilica of St. George
St. Vitus Cathedral
The South Tower
Garden on the Ramparts
The Old Royal Palace
Ludwig´s Wing
The South Garden
Mounted statue of St. George
Monolith of mrakotíne granite
The Golden Gate
The Old Provost´s
Theresian Wing
Chapel of the Holy Cross
Coal Fountain
Dusty Gate
Mathew´s Gate
Gate of the Giants
Archbishop´s Palace

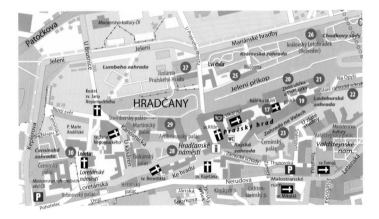

Around Prague Castle, Hradčany

pp. 132 – C1, C2

The Royal Crypt was built at the end of the 16th century into the remains of the Romanesque buildings of the St. Vitus Chapter House. Its present-day appearance is the result of renovations made in the early 20th century. Pride of place belongs to Charles IV († 1378), but his son Wenceslas IV († 1419) is also buried here with his spouse Johanna of Bavaria as well as Kings Ladislav Pohrobek († 1457), George of Poděbrady († 1471) and Rudolph II. († 1612), who is stored in his original, richly decorated tin coffin.

After the death of Petr Parléř in 1399, building work slowed down, and after the outbreak of the Hussite Wars in 1420, it stopped completely. Over the following centuries, only the cathedral was completed. The Late Gothic **Royal Oratory** was built in 1493 in tribute to the Jagiellonians.

The Renaissance-styled **Royal Mausoleum** with the graves of Ferdinand I, Anna and Maxmilian II was built in the late 16th century during the reign of Habsburg dynasty.

The **silver tombstone of Jan of Nepomuk** that decorates the Baroque cathedral was completed with allegorical statues and angels in 1746.

Work on the completion of the cathedral continued well into the 20th century. The decoration of the cathedral became an opportunity for modern Czech artists to show their abilities. Josef

The Golden Gate – detail of the mosaic of the Last Judgement 15

25

The open space in front of the Convent of St. George

Václav Myslbek's **Tomb of Cardinal B. Schwarzenberk**, completed in 1895, was granted an award in Paris in 1900. Regarding modern works, the original Art Nouveau **symbolic altars** by the sculptor František Bílek, or the **stained glass window displays** [14] by famous Czech artists (i.a. Alfons Mucha, Max Švabinský) are certainly captivating.

THE CONVENT OF ST. GEORGE, VIKÁŘSKÁ AND JIŘSKÁ STREET

The Benedictine **Convent of St. George** [16] ranks amongst the oldest standing buildings of Prague Castle. The Baroque facade of its church conceals a basilica from the year 920, founded by the father of St. Wenceslas – Vratislav I. Today the

The Renaissance Tympanum of the Basilica of St. George

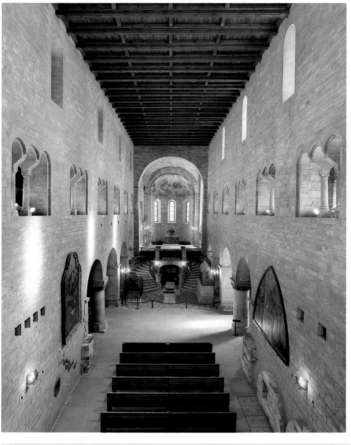

The Basilica of St. George (founded in 915)

National Gallery and its collections of Rudolphine and Baroque art are situated in the convent complex.

The Interior of the Basilica of St. George [17] is the result of alterations from the middle of the 12th century. The convent, founded in 973, is the oldest monastery in the country and served as an educational institution for genteel Bohemians. Přemyslid princes are buried in the convent church, including the founder of the church Vratislav I († 921) and his mother, St. Ludmila († 921) – the grandmother of St. Wenceslas. The vault chevet of the main nave and the vault ends of both side naves are decorated with Late Romanesque paintings from the first half of the 13th century.

The Renaissance-styled southern portal of St.George's Basilica has a **tympanum with St. George slaying the dragon [18]**.

Vikářská ulice (Vikářská Street) joins to the northern side of Jiřské náměstí (St. George's Square). From here, you can walk along to the northern fortification with the **Mihulka** artillery **Tower**

Jiřská Lane **(19)**

built at the end of the 15th century. Suprisingly, it never served any military purpose. During the reign of Rudolph II, alchemists kept their workshops here. Later, gunpowder was stored here, causing an explosion in 1645. Luckily, the tower was so well-built that it remained standing.

Jiřská Lane (St. George's Lane) **[19]** slopes down around the southern side of the Convent of St. George. The classicist **Institute of Nobles** runs down Jiřská Lane opposite St. George's Basilica. Built in 1753, on the site of the Renaissance styled Rožmberk Palace, Jiřská Lane runs along the length of the Lobkowitz Palace,

Golden Lane **(20)**

where you will find a National Museum exhibition, and the Renaissance-styled buildings of the Highest Burgrave, built in 1555, to the Black Tower.

The extensively restored premises of the medieval seat of government, **The Highest Burgrave**, boast interiors with perfectly preserved Renaissance fittings. The Romanesque **Black Tower [21]**, built in 1135, served as a prison. The Renaissance **East Gate** from 1560, stands beside the Black Tower and opens onto the **Old Chateau Steps [22]** in the direction of the Malá Strana (Lesser Town) and to the **Opyš**, where there is a wonderful viewing terrace on the site of the original fortification, and from where, at one time, a canon shot announced midday to the citizens of Prague.

You can turn from Jiřská Lane onto the picturesque **Zlatá ulička (Golden Lane) [20]**. This attractive Renaissance styled quarter, connected to the castle fortifications, gives us a view of what the lodgings for castle servants and

The Black Tower

personnel probably looked like. From 1591, "useless menials", as well as castle marksmen and later, goldsmiths, lived here. **Franz Kafka** stayed here for a short time between 1916 and 1917.

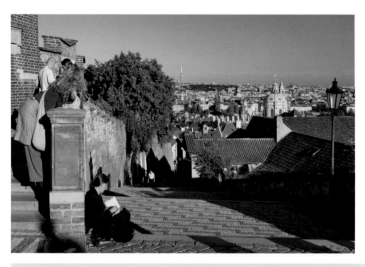

The old chateau steps (access to the Castle from the Lesser Town station – Malostranská) **22**

South Gardens – Bellevue Pavilion

THE PRAGUE CASTLE GARDENS

Gardens spread out in the area immediately surrounding Prague Castle. They have been growing here from as early as 1534, during the reign of Ferdinand I. They conceal a series of Renaissance and Baroque statues by eminent artists and noteworthy buildings, such as the 17th century Baroque **Riding Hall [27]**. Since 1948, it has been an exhibition hall.

Situated in the Royal Garden, The Renaissance **Ball Game Pavilion [25]**,

South Gardens – Round Dish (J. Plečnik)

The Ball Game Pavilon (Míčovna) is richly decorated with Renaissance sgraffito (1567– 1569) **25**

built in 1569, is the oldest walled sports hall in Europe. In 1557, the first tulips north of the Alps bloomed in the Royal Garden and from here, they found their way to Holland.

Modern-day artist, Eva Jiřičná created the **New Orangery**, a modern technical wonder, between 1995 and 1998, on the original foundations of the Rudolphine orangery, dating from the 17th century.

The Renaissance **Folly of Queen Anne Jagiellon** [26] is the most famous building in the gardens of Prague Castle. Ferdinand I had it built for his wife in the Royal Gardens in the mid-16th century. Decorated with dozens of Renaissance styled historical- and courtesan-themed reliefs, it was, in its day, the most Italianate building north of the Alps. Water, spurting from the bronze **Singing Fountain** made in 1564, tinkles in front of the Folly.

The South Garden and connecting **Na Valech garden** [23] are also worthy of attention. These gardens underwent many changes from the time of their foundation in 1559. Their present appearance corresponds to alterations carried out in the 1920s: the main entrance is from Hradčany Square, but the **Bull steps** also connect them to the Third Courtyard. The garden ornaments include a sizable circular **Bowl** [24]

Nocturnal Allegory (1734)

Queen Anne's Folly

made from a single piece of granite, a **marl pyramid** and a series of viewing pavilions (**Bellevue [23]**) as well as varied architectural and sculptural designs from Baroque to modern times. Two sandstone **obelisks** mark the spot where the vice-regents landed after their defenestration in 1618. They were surprisingly unharmed by the fall. The Protestant chronicler, Pavel Skála of Zhoř, attributed their survival to a pile of manure located in the spot; Catholics attributed their survival as assistance from winged angels or the Virgin Mary.

Riding Hall

Hradčany Square with Salmov Palace on the right

HRADČANY

Hradčany, settled since the 3rd millennium B.C., spreads out to the west of Prague Castle. Around 1320, a medieval town was built, and in 1598, Hradčany was first granted municipal privileges. Hradčany was not a typical town. Diminutive burgher houses from the 14th century huddle in the **Lesser Town (Malá Strana)** in the shadow of the palaces. Today, these houses, with their simpler Renaissance and Early Baroque facades, contrast with the noble monumentality of the palaces, creating a poetic magic.

Archbishop´s Palace

Loreta – *every hour one can hear unique chimes from the end of the 17th century* **30**

At its centre is **Hradčanské náměstí (Hradčany Square)** [28], which opens onto the main entrance of the first courtyard of Prague Castle. Grand palace courts and ecclesiastical institutions decorate the square, such as the Renaissance **Lobkowicz** (later called **Schwarzenberg**) **Palace** built with sgraffito decoration completed in 1563, in which the Military Museum now has an exhibition. The gate leading to the Šternberk Palace leads us around

Strahov Monastery (1143) – Its unique collections contain a picture gallery and library. **31**

www.loreta.cz   www.strahovskyklaster.cz

Around Prague Castle, Hradčany and the Lesser Town

p. 132 – C1, C2, D1, D2

the corner to the Rococo facade of the **Archbishop's Palace [29]**, which contains the very valuable European art collections of the **National Gallery**.

Besides the gracious noble palaces and their luxurious gardens, such as the Černín Palace garden, churches such as the exquisite **Loreta [30]** (1626; baroque facing of the complex by K. I. Dienzenhofer, dating from 1722), dominate Hradčany.

THE STRAHOV MONASTERY, PETŘÍN AND MALÁ STRANA (THE LESSER TOWN)

The **Strahov Monastery [31]**, founded in the mid-12th century, spreads out to the south of Hradčany. Frequently reconstructed throughout its history, its Baroque face is the most distinctive, but the Rudolphine **Church of St. Roch**, dating from the 17th century is also worthy of attention as well as the Romanesque walls of the monastery buildings. The above indicates the

complexity of the building development of this district. The spacious buildings today serve as part of the Monastery, **The Museum of Czech Literature** and the rich **Strahov Gallery**. The library, containing thousands of books

Petřín View-Tower

Vrtbovská Garden

Wallenstein Garden **34**

and manuscripts, the oldest of which date from the 9th century, is especially noteworthy. The bookcases in the Theological and Philosophical Halls, built in Baroque style in the late 17th century, are original.

The Strahov Monastery is connected to the **Petřín Orchards**, located on the remains of the original hunting grounds. In the 12th century, vineyards and gardens took over the grounds and today, a two-kilometre long walking path runs through Petřín, offering a view from the **Petřín View Tower [32]**, a 60 m high copy of the Paris Eiffel Tower. In addition, there is a curious mirror **Labyrinth**, which, like Petřín, was made in celebration of the Jubilee exhibitions in 1891. There are also dozens of statues or groups of statues and a **funicular railway** that takes you to the top of Petřín Hill.

Malá Strana (Lesser Town) can be found in the area under Petřín and Prague Castle. In the 8th century, a mercantile settlement existed for a few hundred years, until Prince Břetislav moved the Jewish settlers to the other

The extensive residence of Albrecht of Wallenstein was built during 1624–1630 **35**

Malostranské náměstí (square), the steeple of the Church of St. Thomas is in the background

side of the Vltava in the 11th century. The Lesser Town became the residential town for Bohemian nobility and foreign envoys. Perhaps not surprisingly, this is the home to many embassies today.

The Lesser Town obtained municipal privileges from Přemysl Otakar II in 1257. Its centre at that time was

Malostranské náměstí (Lesser Town Square) [32] with the **Church of St. Nicholas** [38]. St. Nicholas Church and its adjacent Jesuit College represents the most monumental religious building of the Prague Baroque.

The originally Protestant Church of the Most Holy Trinity, handed over to the

The Lesser Town – Mostecká Street

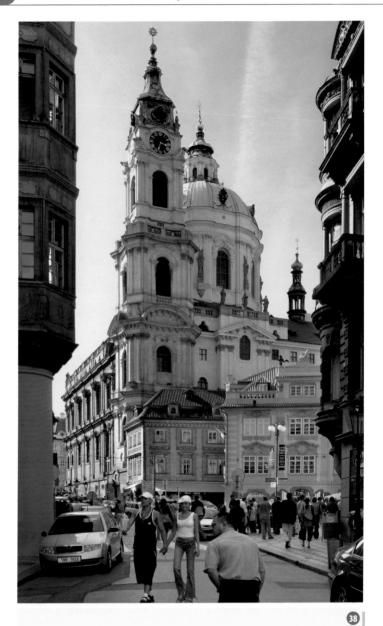

38

The Church of St. Nicholas

A dominant feature of the Lesser Town, the 79 m high Church of St. Nicholas, is one of the foremost central European Baroque monuments. Christopher Dienzenhofer, a German builder who worked in Bohemia, and his son Kilián Ignác, who continued with his father's work, created it. The Jesuits commissioned the building on the site of an older church. Works of Baroque masters are represented in the richly decorated interiors. The adjacent bell tower, which signalled the outbreak of fires, is the last warning tower in Prague. Wolfgang Amadeus Mozart played in the church on his visits. The cathedral and the tower are accessible today.

The Church of St. Nicholas

Catholics after the lost uprising and dedicated to **Our Lady of Victory** [39], was the first Baroque church in Prague. In 1628, it became the home of the **Miraculous Infant Jesus of Prague**.

The Augustinian **St. Thomas Church** [36] conceals a Baroque treasure in the shape of an altar by Peter Paul Rubens, commissioned in 1636. This altar is accessible to the public.

The magnificence of baroque palaces, such as Thunovský Palace built in 1726 in Nerudova Street, and the charm of baroque gardens such as the **Vrtbovská Garden** [33] with statues from 1730, or the Ledeburská Garden made in 1720, attracted many dignitaries such as Prince Albrecht of Wallenstein. He made use of the Post-White Mountain confiscation of Protestant Property to build his imposing residence of 22 houses, a brickworks and several gardens to form the **Albrecht of Wallenstein Palace** [35, 35] in the early 17th century. Today, it is the

Lesser Town residential signs

Residential signs made in the 14th century decorate the historic houses in the Lesser Town and other historic parts of Prague. This system survived until 1770, when house numbers were introduced. The signs were most often made in plaster or painted on the facade, and used as advertisements for goldsmiths, violin makers or apothecaries. The great variety of displayed symbols gave the houses names that found their way into the public consciousness. Here are some examples from buildings in Nerudova Street: U Dvou slunců (At the Two Suns), U Tří housliček (At the Three Little Violins), U Zlaté číše (At the Golden Goblet), U Tří pštrosů (At the Three Ostriches) and so on.

home of the Czech House of Parliament. The Swedes plundered the wonderful Wallenstein garden, decorated with bronze statues made by Adrien de Vries, in 1648. The original statues are now in Drottningholm, Sweden; what you see are copies.

Nerudova Street in the Lesser Town

The local aristocratic residences were considerably more modest before Albrecht's of Wallenstein' time, such as the **Smiřický Palace** on Malostranské Náměstí (Lesser Town Square), with its partially-altered façade dating from after 1763. The **Šternberk Palace**, located next to the Smiřický Palace suffered from a terrible fire that started in 1541, badly damaging The Lesser Town, and Prague Castle.

The Johannine **Church of the Virgin Mary under the Chain** [40], dating from 1169, is probably the most impressive of Lesser Town structures. Its Gothic hall and tower appears in front of the remains of the Romanesque walls, behind which the presbytery was converted in Baroque style. The Knights of St. John, known as the Maltese Knights after 1530, were supposed to protect the stone bridge.

The Church of the Victorious Virgin Mary **39**
(in the foreground)
and the Virgin Mary under the Chain **40**
(in the middle)

Charles Bridge at dawn

THE CHARLES BRIDGE, VLTAVA, PRAGUE BRIDGES AND ISLANDS

In 1169, Prague already had a stone bridge, named **Judith Bridge** in honour of the wife of King Vladislav I. It stood roughly on the site of the present-day Charles Bridge, but it was lower, had more arches and was longer, because it pointed more in the direction of the flow of the river from the Lesser Town bank. The **Lesser Town Bridge Gate**, built on the site of a 12th century Romanesque tower, still respects the angle of the original Judith Bridge and is thus somewhat out of sync with the Charles Bridge. The Judith Bridge was swept away by a flood in 1342 and so Charles IV had a new stone bridge – **The Charles Bridge** – built from 1357 [41]. Its outstanding construction relates the genius of Petr Parléř. The bridge is 520 metres long by 10 metres wide, and sixteen arches support it. The bridge pillars form the bases for **sculptural decoration**. Now the bridge is decorated with twenty eight sculptures, mainly dating from the Baroque period.

The oldest preserved statue on the Charles Bridge is **St. John Nepomuk** [42] from 1683. It stands on the spot from where his body was thrown into the river.

Charles Bridge

The most famous bridge in Bohemia was built in 1357 by Charles IV on the site of the older Judith Bridge, which had been destroyed by a flood. Prague's most visited monument, it has survived natural disasters and the turmoil of war over the centuries. The statues of Charles Bridge look down on the citizens of Prague and tourists from all over the world who stroll and pause beside the musicians, painters and souvenir sellers.

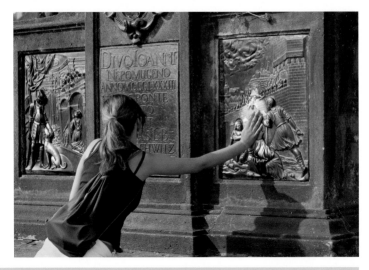

Reliefs on the base of the statue of St. John Nepomuk (touching them apparently brings luck) **42**

The cult of this saint and the custom of placing his statues on bridges spread out from here.

The ecclesiastical orders and the university faculties competed with each other in the magnificence of their celebrations of their holy protectors.

On the Old Town riverbank, the bridge ends at the **Old Town Bridge Tower** **[44]**, which boasts rich decoration from the 1380s. Depictions of the reigning Charles IV, his son Wenceslas IV, and their kingdom under the protection of the country's saints, lead the eye to another aspect of their era with disgraceful scenes on the cornices on the ground floor of the tower.

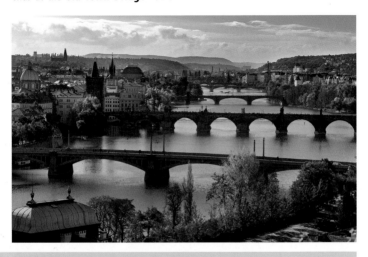

The Vltava river with the Prague bridges

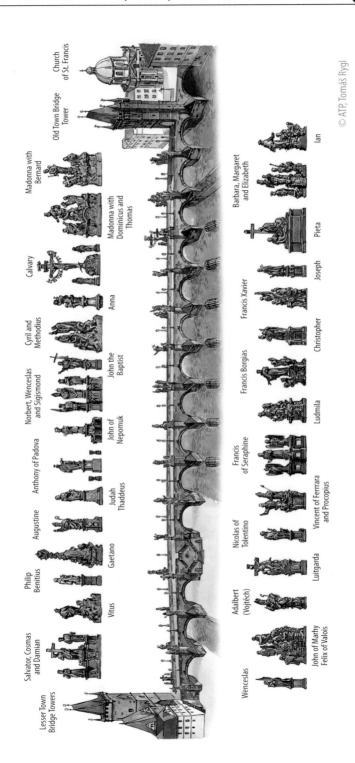

© ATP, Tomáš Rygl

Not even in winter does Prague lose anything of its magical atmosphere...

The small, but picturesque **Kampa island** [43] spreads out by the Lesser Town river bank under the arches of the Charles Bridge. Like the Lesser Town, it is full of ostentatious palaces, beautiful gardens and parks, but also romantic nooks, where you will perhaps meet figures from old Prague fairytales or ghosts.

. . . view of the Charles Bridge and the Castle from the river bank

Eight islands stretch through Prague along the Vltava. Apart from Kampa, the main one is **Slav Island** (originally Barvířský, later called Žofín until 1918) – a centre of social life. Concerts by Liszt, Berlioz and Tchaikovsky were played on in the restaurant in the early 19th century. In 1848, the Slav Congress took place here, attended by representatives of all the Slavic nations, but revolution

Prague of a "Hundred Spires"

Prague's many epithets – The Mother of Cities (Praga mater urbium), The Head of the Kingdom (Praga caput regni), Golden Prague, A Pearl amongst Cities, The Heart of Europe, Rome of the North and Prague of a Hundred spires – all relate to Prague's glory. Prague, however, has more than one thousand. Here is the view of the Old Town Bridge Tower in the Old Town; in the middle we can see the gable of the Church of St. Salvador.

broke out before they could agree on anything.

It is possible to sail in tourist boats along the Vltava today, but the more able-bodied can hire pedal boats and romantically paddle amongst the Prague weirs. The average depth of the Vltava is around 2.5 m.

STARÉ MĚSTO (THE OLD TOWN) AND THE JEWISH QUARTER

The Old Town, or Staré Město, is the oldest and richest Prague quarter. Its international market, operating here since the 9th century, earned the admiration of the Jewish merchant and chronicler, Ibrahim Ibn Jakob, in 965. At that time, the centre was most likely located near the river on the site of an old ford, on the edge of the Jewish quarter, where Palackého náměstí (square) is today and by the Mánes Bridge ford. In the 11th century, the centre moved south and it has remained there to this day – on the Old Town Square. Medieval Prague used to be very cosmopolitan. German traders settled to the north and north-east of the square, merchants from Romance countries to the south and south-east, Czechs to the east of the square and Jews to the north-west.

Čertovka, a dead meander in the Vltava, passes through the mysterious Kampa

Old Town Bridge Tower

44

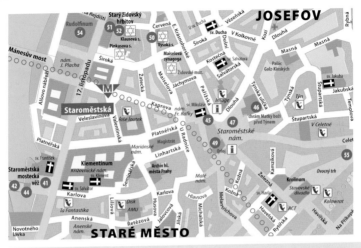

Staré Město (the Old Town) – the surroundings of the Old Town Square   **p. 133 – D3, D4**

More than seventy of the oldest preserved Romanesque **stone houses** lie along the streets of the Old Town, a unique feat in central Europe. The **Palace of the Lords of Kunštát** ranks amongst the most well-known. The foundations have survived to the present thanks to the artificially-raised ground of around 7 m, which were required in the 13th century after the construction of weirs on the Vltava. Rafts transported wood along these waterways from as far away as the Šumava Forest.

Mary's Column, Mariánský sloup, was built on the **Old Town Square** [47] on the site of the Prague Meridian in 1680. This column also served as a sundial, and suffered damage during the Proclamation of the Czechoslovakian Republic in 1918. The **Jan Hus Memorial**, created in Art Nouveau style in 1915, depicts the founder of the Czech Reformation.

Just around the corner we'll find the **Kinský Palace**, one of the most beautiful Prague Rococo buildings built in 1765; it

now houses the **graphic collections of the National Gallery**.

The picturesque **Týn School** with arcades from the 13th century, and the main **Church of our Lady in front of Týn** [46] looming behind it stands beside the Romanesque **House of the Stone Bell**,

Street musicians add colour to the Prague streets

53

St. Nicholas Church in the Old Town

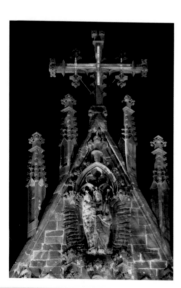

Tympanum of the Gothic Cathedral of the Virgin Mary in front of Týn

converted during the Gothic period. Many medieval rulers resided in the Bell House, and in the 14th century, Petr Parléř built the main part of the Church of our Lady. This church became a centre of Bohemian Utraquism, whose doctrine decreed that Man, in order to be saved, must receive Holy Communion when and where he wishes. The church houses perfectly preserved medieval sculptural decorations and the tomb stone of famous astronomer Tycho Brahe.

Standing behind Týn Church, the **Ungelt** building served as Bohemia's customs house and business centre in the 11th century. Later, in the 16th century, Ferdinand I gave it to the burgher Jakub Granovský, who had the Ungelt

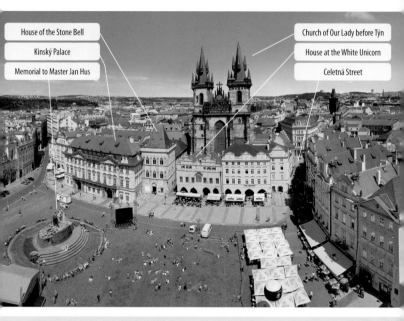

House of the Stone Bell

Kinský Palace

Memorial to Master Jan Hus

Church of Our Lady before Týn

House at the White Unicorn

Celetná Street

Old Town Square (Staroměstské náměstí) **47**

converted into a Renaissance municipal palace around 1560.

The remains of the **Town Hall with Chapel and Tower** date from the 14th century and stand on the western side of Old Town Square. Crosses in the pavement of Old Town Square commemorate the execution of twenty seven leaders during the Rising of the Estates from 1618. The actual building of the Old Town Hall comprises several burgher houses that were eventually connected together to build a town hall in 1338.

The still functional **Astronomical clock** **[49]** decorates the southern façade of the town hall. Mikuláš of Kadaň built it in 1410, but Master Hanuš later improved it in 1490. The Astronomical clock has been repaired many times since then. In 1864, Josef Mánes, the most famous artist of the Czech National Revival, created

calendar panel for the astronomical clock.

The German army destroyed the Neo-Gothic part of the city hall during the Prague Uprising in May 1945. This opened

Štorch House **48**

55

Old Town Square

a view onto the **St. Nicholas Church** [45] built by K. I. Dienzenhofer in 1735. The remaining structures from the old Jewish Ghetto, demolished in 1896, include the **Old-New Synagogue** [50] from the 13th century, the oldest preserved synagogue in central Europe, and the exceptional **Jewish Cemetery** [51, 52] that was in use between the 15th and 18th centuries. Amongst the twenty thousand gravestones, you can find the grave of the celebrated Rabbi Löwe, reputed to have created the legendary Golem – an artificial man – here during the Rudolphine era. The rich collections

of the Jewish Museum document the often troubled history of Judaism in Bohemia. Most of the Jewish quarter made way for Art Nouveau buildings. **Pařížská ulice (Paris Street), in particular, holds The Rudolphinum** [54] and has been a sanctuary of the arts since 1883, when it was built to honour the visit of Crown Prince Rudolph, son of Emperor Franz Joseph. Josef Zítek and Josef Schulz, chief architects of the Czech National Theatre, built it.

Founded by Agnes Přemyslid in 1234 for Franciscans and Poor Clares, the most famous of the Old Town monasteries,

Old Town City Hall with the Astronomical Clock
Founded as the administrative centre of the Old Town in 1338, the Old Town City Hall is actually a row of Gothic houses, whose history stretch back to Romanesque times. The 66 m high tower, dating from 1364, is one of the most significant Prague attractions with the Astronomical Clock located on its southern side. Created by Mikuláš of Kadaň and Jan Šindel in 1410, a bustling mechanical performance has taken place every hour for hundreds of years. As the twelve apostles walk around in two windows, a skeleton pulls a bell on a string and after the crowing of a cock the clock mechanism starts to chime the hour. The Astronomical Clock has four main moving components: the zodiacal ring, an outer rotating ring, an icon representing the Sun, and an icon representing the Moon.

Ceremonial Hall at the Jewish Cemetery

The Old-New Synagogue
Built in the 13th century, the Old-New Synagogue is the oldest preserved synagogue in Europe and remains the most valuable historic monument in the Jewish Quarter. The synagogue is associated with many legends, especially the legend of Golem, an artificial man created by Rabbi Löwe in the 16th century that was hidden in a secret place in the attic of the synagogue. After walking around Josefov, we recommend refreshments in **Les Moules café restaurant** *on Pařížská Street.*

St. Agnes Convent [53] on Na Františku, holds the impressive **Collection of Medieval Art** of the National Gallery.

The Štorch House [48], with frescoes by Mikoláš Aleš in a style that links Art Nouveau with the Neo-Renaissance tradition of the National revival, stands on the boundary of Old Town Square and Celetná Street. A jewel of modern architecture made between 1909 and 1911 – the **Cubist House at the Black Mother of God** [55] by Josef Gočár majestically spreads

Old Jewish Cemetery

Convent of St. Agnes

www.jewishmuseum.cz

www.ngprague.cz

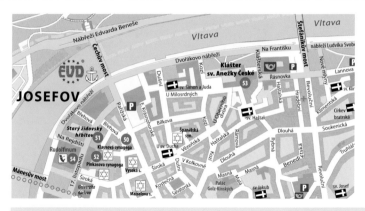

Josefov – The Jewish Quarter and surrounding area　　　　**p. 133 – C3, C4**

out in the middle of Celetná Street on the corner of the Fruit Market.

The Classicist building of the Stavovské Theatre dominates the Fruit Market and witnessed the celebrated premiere of Mozart's Don Giovanni in 1787.

A diverse complex of university buildings bordering on Celetná Street form **the Carolinum** [56]. They are mainly clad with facades from the Baroque or 19th century, but many interiors conceal a Gothic core. Charles University, the oldest in central Europe, was founded by Charles IV in 1348. The core of the whole block is the Rothlev Building, which Wenceslas IV gave to the university in 1383. Since 1611, the rectory of the university has remained here.

Celetná Street runs into the Late Gothic **Prašná brána (Powder Gate)** [57]

Rudolphinum (1876–1885), the seat of the Czech Philharmonic Orchestra

House at the Black Mother of God- a perfect example of Cubist architecture **55**

built in 1475. This structure clearly illustrates how the Jagiellonians wished to compete with the Luxembourg dynasty. The Powder Gate nearly adjoins The Royal Court, which used to be the favourite private residence of Bohemian rulers. Later, it became the **Obecní dům (Municipal House)** **[57]**. Built in 1911, this is a perfect example of Prague Art Nouveau, and is still a lively cultural centre that features many highly acclaimed exhibits.

Carolinum – the seat of Charles University founded by Charles IV in 1348 **56**

Late Gothic Powder Gate and Art Nouveau Municipal House **57**

The **Coronation Path of the Bohemian Kings** runs through the western and south-western parts of the Old Town and connects Vyšehrad Castle with Prague. The Romanesque **Rotunda of the Holy Cross [59]** from the 11th century is one of the many treasures that are to be found along this way.

The Bethlehem Chapel [60], originally built in 1391, demolished in 1786, and rebuilt in 1953, was where the reformer Jan Hus preached.

Built on Křížovnické Náměstí (Křížovnické Square) in 1556, a Jesuit college, later called the **Clementinum** in honour of St. Clement Cathedral, grew into an extensive complex following the Thirty Years' War. The Baroque-styled interiors of the cathedral with its Mirror Chapel or the Library and Mathematical Hall, illustrate the development of Baroque art in Bohemia in the early 19th century. The Clementinum also served as a library. The present-day National Library continues this tradition, containing more than six million volumes and a large collection of precious medieval manuscripts.

The **San Salvador Church**, part of the Clementinum, connects to the **Italian Chapel [58]**. Built from 1590 to 1597,

Vlašská (Italian) Chapel **58**

Rotunda of the Holy Cross **59**

it is the oldest European cathedral built on an elliptical ground plan. Italian architects of the time could only dream of what their Italian colleagues put into practice during the reign of Rudolf II.

Wenceslas I founded **Havelské město (Havel's town)** in 1234. Originally designed to be an isolated new market place, its privileges also expanded to cover the older settlement. Havel's town became the main municipal market place and it still serves this function

Bethlehem Chapel **60**

today. During the reign of Charles IV, a gigantic basilica served as a kind of medieval department store in this area. The remains of its central nave on V Kotcích Street are lined with Gothic arcades, where you will still find a permanent market.

NOVÉ MĚSTO (THE NEW TOWN)

Charles IV founded Nové Město (the New Town) in 1348, although people were already living here as early as the 10th century. Unlike the cosmopolitan Old Town, the New Town was mainly inhabited by Czech burghers who regarded themselves as craftsmen. The rivalry of both Prague towns influenced history until their official joining in 1784. The medieval outline of the New Town was incredibly far ahead of its time by several centuries, containing 360 hectares of land within the rampart boundaries demarcated by Charles IV. Its streets, up to twenty seven metres wide in places, imposed order on the chaotic scattering of settlements, and were suitable for traffic until the second half of the 20th century.

German merchants settled around the Romanesque **Church of St. Peter** from the 12th century. The Church was rebuilt in Gothic style between the 14th and 15th centuries. From time immemorial, it was called Poříčí (river basin) and the main local street – Na Poříčí – was named after it. **Na Poříčí** is dominated by the celebrated Cubist **Legiobank** building **[61]** built by Josef Gočár in 1923, a good example of unique Czech Cubist architecture.

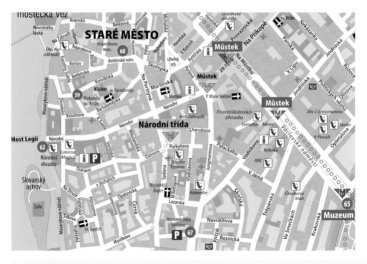

Old and New Town – around Národní třída (National Avenue)   **p. 133, 137 – D3, D4**

After the demolition of the Old Town ramparts in the 1780s, a circular grand avenue (in three parts: now called Revoluční, Na Příkopech and Národní) was built in their place above the filled-in castle moat. This avenue connects with Na Poříčí Street at **náměstí Republiky (Republic Square)** A dominant feature of Náměstí Republiky is not only the Municipal House and Powder Gate, but also the **House at the Hibernians**, an Empire building customs house named after the local monastery of Irish Franciscans.

The dominant feature of Národní třída and the embankment is the **National Theatre [62]**, built by Josef Zítek with monies donated from generous patrons and the common people. After the conflagration in 1881, Josef Schulz repaired it. Important artists of the day participated in its decoration. The Neo-Renaissance style gradually changed into Art Nouveau.

Dating from the end of the 15th century, the **Water Tower** stands within sight of the National Theatre opposite the banks of Slav Island, and incorporated Late Gothic and Functionalist styles in 1930

Legiobanka

Národní divadlo (National Theatre)

The greatest show of nationalism of the 19th century was the building of the National Theatre by architect Josef Zítek, inspired by the North Italian Renaissance. The National Theatre celebrated its opening in 1881 with a performance of Smetana's Libuše. After an extensive fire broke out, the theatre had to be rebuilt, this time by architect Josef Schultz in 1883. The most distinguished Bohemian artists of the day, later known as the "National Theatre Generation," decorated the theatre. One of the first theatre buildings in Europe to boast electrical lighting, it remains a unique display of 19th century Bohemian art.

to create the modern building of the **Mánes Artists' Association**.

The noteworthy **Dancing House** [63] built by Croatian architect Vlado Milunić and American architect Frank O. Gehry in 1996, breathes new life onto the Vltava riverbank.

Václavské Náměstí (Wenceslas Square) [65] was until 1848 a horse market, but became the main centre of modern Prague from the second half of the 19th century. Its magnificent medieval dimensions, occupying an area of 41 400 square metres, fully suit the needs of modern times. The imposing houses and palaces of Wenceslas Square illustrate the development of Czech modern architecture with The National Museum as its dominant feature.

The National Museum [65], a Neo-Renaissance building built in 1890 by Josef Schulz, was not intended to be a mere museum, but a centre of Czech sciences and cultural and political ambitions. The allegorical sculptures depicting the Czech lands and Czech rivers and its lavish interiors conceal rich collections, and Pantheon hall dedicated to the memory of exceptional personalities from the Czech lands.

www.narodni-divadlo.cz

Dancing House 63

In front of the National Museum in the upper part of Wenceslas Square stands the **St. Wenceslas Equestrian Memorial [65]**, built in 1924 by the founder of modern Czech sculpture J. V. Myslbek. Its Baroque predecessor dates from 1680 and is located in the Lapidarium. This memorial depicts the main protector of the Czech lands accompanied by his grandmother St. Ludmila, St. Prokop, St. Agnes of Bohemia and Bishop St. Vojtěch. The citizens of Prague gather under this monument for amorous meetings or political demonstrations, as exemplified by the demonstrations against communism that convened here in 1989.

The Romanesque **Rotunda of St. Longin [64]** from the 11th century stands a short way from the Parish Church of St. Stephen here. The Church of St. Stephen used to be the parish church of the settlement called Rybníček, hence, Na Rybníčku Street.

Žitná Street runs from St. Stephen's to what was once a livestock market, now known as **Karlovo Náměstí (Charles**

Rotunda of St. Longin 64

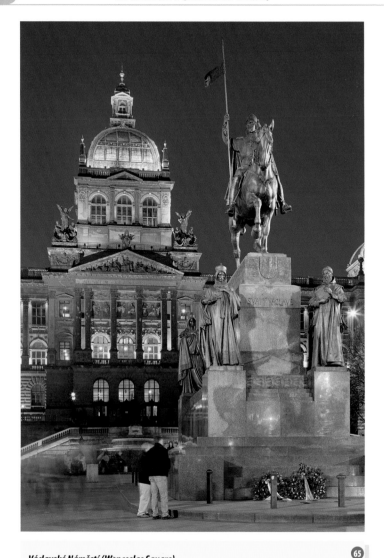

Václavské Náměstí (Wenceslas Square) 65

Wenceslas Square, founded in 1348 as the centre of the New Town was quite exceptional in the 14th century due to its immense size. Known as the Horse Market until the mid 19th century, its social significance increased, evolving into a venue where significant events in Czech culture and politics took place. Important buildings such as the National Museum were built at the top of the square in 1890. The bronze equestrian sculpture of Vaclav (St. Wenceslas) sits majestically atop the square, accompanied by four Czech patron saints: St. Ludmilla, St. Agnes, St. Adalbert and St. Prokop. Today, Wenceslas Square is the centre of Prague life, lined with shops, fast-food eateries, hotels, theatres, and cinemas.

Square) [67]. Covering 80,500 square metres, Charles IV founded it as the main centre of new Prague. The **New Town City Hall** [67] is also located here, serving its purpose until 1784. The building of the town hall, built from 1377 to 1418, bore witness to the first Czech Defenestration in 1419, during which aldermen involuntarily left their functions and offices, and this world. Their deaths were the cause of Wenceslas IV's heart attack; the king's demise then set off the avalanche of the Hussite Wars.

The monumental Baroque **Church of St. Ignatius**, completed in 1670 stands centred on the eastern side of Charles Square, and is a part of the extensive Jesuit College now the Teaching Hospital of Charles University. The church interiors are mainly Rococo.

Resslova Street runs from the façade of St. Ignatius down to the river. Its dominant feature is

The Art Nouveau Topič salon

the Baroque **Cathedral of St. Cyril and Methodius**, built in 1736. In 1942, Czechoslovakian parachutists carried out the assassination of a Reichsprotektor, hid in its crypt, and died.

Villa America (K. I. Dienzenhofer, 1712–20) – is now the Antonín Dvořák Museum 66

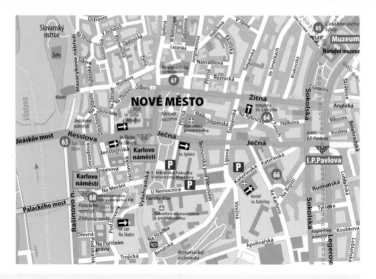

New Town – around Karlovo náměstí (Charles Square) **p. 137 – E3,E4**

Emause Monastery [68] is located south of Karlovo Náměstí (Charles Square). Built between 1347 and 1372, it is the only new building to have been completed in Charles IV's lifetime, and exceptional care was taken in its decoration. A unique cycle of frescoes complements this beautiful, treble-nave monastery church. These frescoes represent the largest preserved group of medieval wall paintings outside Italy. The monastery, destroyed by bombing at the end of the Second World War was given a new roof in 1967, and this bold

New Town City Hall on Karlovo Náměstí (Charles Square) **67**

Church of St. John Nepomuk on the Cliff and the Emause Monastery　68

construction became the new dominant feature of the embankment.

The beautiful Gothic **Church of St. Apollinaris** from the second half of the 14th century looks down from above to the centre of the New Town towards Karlovo náměstí (Charles Square). Gothic wall paintings from the end of the 14th century and a rich Baroque interior, including a painting of the Virgin Mary of Karlovská, the patroness of pregnant women, have been preserved here. There is, in fact, a maternity hospital nearby.

The admirable, eight-sided Cathedral of the Augustinian Capitulary, dedicated to the **Virgin Mary and Charlemagne**, is located in Na Karlově. Charles IV intended this building to recall Charlemagne's Chapel at Aachen as he regarded himself as the great Emperor's successor. The present-day cupola is Renaissance styled, dating from 1575. Its gigantic star vault deliberately evokes the distant past, joining Renaissance and Gothic historicism together.

Designed as a French type suburban villa, the baroque-styled **Villa America** [66] dates from 1712 and was decorated with statues made around 1730. Since 1932, it has housed the Antonín Dvořák Museum.

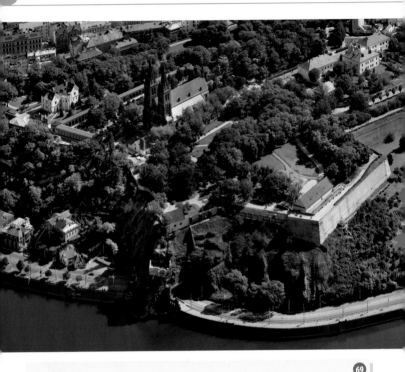

Vyšehrad [69]

Few places in the Czech Republic are associated with as many tales and legends as Vyšehrad, where we can trace the origin of Čech, the great forefather of the Czechs. The descendants of his tribe were the Přemyslids, founded by Přemysl the Ploughman. Princess Libuše ruled her people from Vyšehrad until she took Přemysl as her husband after the men had refused to submit to a female ruler. It was here at Vyšehrad, where she uttered her prophecies about the future fame of Prague. The reality, however, was a little different. The hill on the right bank of the Vltava was indeed already settled in the stone age, but Přemyslid castle was founded at a later date than Prague Castle. It did not become a provisional princely seat until the 11th century, when Vyšehrad's Church of St. Peter and Paul and the Romanesque rotunda of St. Martin were built.

VYŠEHRAD

Vyšehrad dates from the 10th century and is the legendary seat of the Přemyslid princes. Although it is newer than Prague Castle, this does not detract from its significance. It reached its period of greatest glory in the second half of the 11th century. At that time, Bohemian King, Vratislav II often resided here as he hated his ambitious brother Jaromír, who was Bishop of Prague. At that time, the king also founded the capitulary **Church of St. Peter and Paul [69]** here. The bishopric lost authority over the church when it was subordinated to the Pope. Its present-day appearance corresponds to the Neo-Gothic period of the 19th century. However, the actual memorial to Vratislav II – the rotunda of St. Martin – is located nearby.

The Rotunda of St. Martin [70] is the oldest preserved Prague rotunda. Today it looks the same as it did in the 11th century.

After the death of Vratislav II, Vyšehrad functioned as Prague's high royal fortress for eight hundred years. Charles IV gave Vyšehrad an opportunity to shine in the 14th century when he incorporated it into his coronation way. The ruler set out from here on his ceremonial symbolic pilgrimage through the town on his way to be crowned King of Bohemia

Rotunda of St. Martin

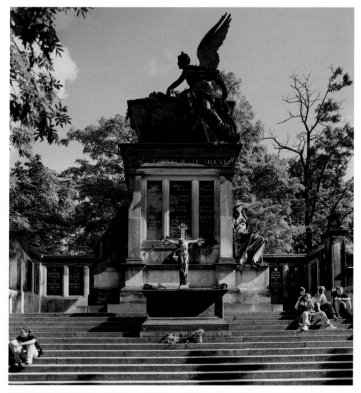

Slavín – the burial place of famous personalities

Cubist Villa by Josef Chochol (1912–14) on the river bank under Vyšehrad

with the crown of St. Wenceslas in the cathedral. Even though Vyšehrad more resembled a craftsman's settlement than a fortification during the 15th century, it retained its symbolic and mythic significance. The 17th century restored its role as a fortress. The interesting **Baroque defences**, completed by 1670, recall a system of ramparts and gates created by Carlo Lurago in the style of North Italian Baroque Classicism.

When the defensive function of Vyšehrad was no longer necessary, the Vyšehrad Cemetary began its expansion in 1866, later becoming the **national cemetery – Slavín** [71]. Architecturally reorganized between 1890 and 1902, this cemetery features the most distinguished personalities from the Czech lands. The **Myslbek group of statues from Palacký Bridge** has stood in the Vyšehrad orchards since 1947, at the site of the Royal Palace. Legendary figures from the past come allegorically to life here.

In the 17th century, the majority of Vyšehrad inhabitants moved into the area under the castle, creating a new municipal district, separated from the New Town by the Botič Stream. The Vyšehrad quarter joined Prague in 1883. Here you will find completely exceptional **Cubist buildings: The Tenement Houses** on Neklanova Street and the **Family Villa** [72] by Josef Chochol built between 1912 and 1914, standing directly under Vyšehrad on the riverbank. These buildings are evidence of the strength and attraction of Cubism here, a new style of modern art reflecting modern life in Bohemia. The First World War, however, interrupted its development and the post-war era brought other worries.

FACTS-AT-A-GLANCE
About the Czech Republic

- **Country name:** Czech Republic
- **System of government:** Parliamentary republic (two chambers), head of state – President
- **Established:** January 1, 1993 (former Czechoslovakia established in 1918)
- **Capital city:** Prague, population: 1.16 million
- **Membership:** EU, UN, Council of Europe, OSCE, NATO
- **Number of inhabitants:** 10.3 million (women 51.3 %, men 48.7 %)
- **Population density:** 131 people / km²
- **Ethnic groups:** Czech (90.4% or 9.25 million); Moravian (more than 380,000); Slovak (193,000); Roma (171,000); Silesian (11,000); Polish (52,000); German (39,000); Ukrainian (22,000); and Vietnamese (18,000)
- **Official language:** Czech
- **Religions:** Roman Catholic, Protestant
- **Average age:** women 77, men 70
- **Average life expectancy:** women 78.5, men 72.3
- **Largest cities:** Prague (1.2 mil. inhabitants), Brno, Ostrava, Plzeň, Olomouc
- **Regions:** The Capital City of Prague, Central Bohemian Region (Prague), South Bohemian Region (České Budějovice), Plzeň Region (Plzeň), Karlovy Vary Region (Karlovy Vary), Ústí nad Labem Region (Ústí nad Labem), Liberec Region (Liberec), Hradec Králové Region (Hradec Králové), Pardubice Region (Pardubice), Vysočina Region (Jihlava),

Karlovy Vary – the most well-known spa water source in our country is Vřídlo (73 °C), its geyser reaches a height of 14 m

South Moravian Region (Brno), Olomouc Region (Olomouc), Moravian-Silesian Region (Ostrava), Zlín Region (Zlín)

- **Area:** 78 864 km²
- **Physical attributes of the country:** landlocked country, mainly made up of hills and highland areas
- **Borders:** total length 2,300 km, with Germany 810 km, with Poland 762 km, with Austria 466 km, with Slovakia 252 km
- **Average temperature:** January: - 3 °C (26.6 F); July: 20-24 °C (68 F)
- **Average height above sea-level:** 430 m
- **Highest point:** Sněžka 1,602 m
- **Lowest point:** Hřensko 116 m
- **Longest rivers:** Vltava 433 km, Elbe 370 km, Dyje 306 km
- **Biggest pond:** Rožmberk 4.89 km²
In the middle ages (16th century) 21,000 ponds in Bohemia, today around a quarter remain
- **Biggest dam:** Lipno 48,7 km²
- **Ground cover:** 33 % forested, 40 % arable land 11 % pasture, 16 % other
- **National Parks:** Czech "Switzerland", Krkonoše (Giant Mountains), Podyjí, Šumava
- **Spas, Spa towns:** Karlovy Vary, Mariánské Lázně, Františkovy Lázně, Teplice, Bílina, Lázně Bělohrad, Poděbrady, Jeseník, Luhačovice

Lipno – the largest body of water in the Czech Republic

- <u>Transport:</u>

a dense railway network (9 454 km), seven major toll motorways

D1: Prague–Brno

D2: Brno–Slovakia

D3: Prague–Tábor–České Budějovice– Austria (under construction)

D5: Prague–Plzeň–Germany

D8: Prague–Ústí nad Labem–Germany

D11: Prague–Hradec Králové–Poland (of 154 km 42 km in operation)

D47: Lipník nad Bečvou–Ostrava–Poland (under construction).

<u>Motorway stickers:</u> p. 80 ►

Czech Switzerland National Park – Pravčická Gate (the largest rock bridge in our country has a span of 26,5 m)

STATE OBSERVED HOLIDAYS:

On these days, public transport is drastically reduced. Bank and state offices are closed.

<u>January 1st</u> – New Year

<u>Easter Monday</u> – a fluctuating holiday – always the first Monday after the first Spring day of Spring, March 21st

<u>May 1st</u> – Labour Day

<u>May 8th</u> – Liberation from Fascism Day

<u>July 5th</u> – Cyril and Methodius Day

<u>July 6th</u> – John Hus Day

<u>September 28th</u> – Day of Czech Nationhood

<u>October 28th</u> – Day of the Foundation of Independent Czechoslovakia

<u>November 17th</u> – The day freedom and democracy were fought for

<u>December 24th</u> – Christmas Eve

<u>December 25th</u> – Christmas Day

<u>December 26th</u> – Boxing Day

STATE SYMBOLS:

- <u>Czech Republic Coat-of-Arms</u> has four fields. The individual fields symbolize the historic lands of the Czech Republic – Bohemia, Moravia and Silesia while the fourth one represents the Republic as a whole. In the upper left, there is a leaping silver double-tailed lion with a gold crown on a red background. In the upper right, a red-silver checked eagle with a gold crown is set on a blue background. In the lower left field, there is a black eagle with red armour and a golden crown on a gold background. A silver half-moon with salient terminated by clover leaves decorates the black eagle. The lower right field repeats the upper left field, with the double-tailed lion.

- <u>The Czech flag:</u> is made up of a blue wedge on the left and a lower red stripe and an upper white stripe

- <u>State colour:</u> white, red and blue

the Czech flag

the Czech coat-of-arms

Kde domov můj?	Where is my home?
/Fr. Škroup – J. K. Tyl (1834)/	/Fr. Škroup - J. K. Tyl (1834)/
Kde domov můj?	Where is my home?
Kde domov můj?	Where is my home?
Voda hučí po lučinách	Water murmurs across meadows
Bory šumí po skalinách	Pinewoods rustle on the rocky heights
V sadě skví se jara květ	Spring blooms burst forth in the orchard
Zemský ráj to na pohled	An earthly paradise to behold
A to je ta krásná země	And that is this beautiful country
Země česká, domov můj	The Czech lands, my home
Země česká, domov můj	The Czech lands, my home

National Anthem

IMPORTANT TELEPHONE NUMBERS:

INFORMATION:

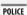 SOS	112	Emergency
	155	Emergency services
POLICE	158	Police
	150	Fire brigade
	156	Municipal police

1230, 1240	Road accident service
12 444	General information
1180	Czech telephone numbers info.
1181, 1188	International tel. numbers info.
133 001	Telephone telegram service

PRAGUE INFORMATION SERVICE:

www.prague-info.cz

tel.: 12 444

- Old Town Square 1 – Old Town City Hall
- Main Railway Station – vestibule
- Rytířská 31, Praha 1
- Lesser Town Bridge Tower (summer months only)

TELEPHONING THE CZECH REPUBLIC

Dialling code + 420 + local number (9-digit number)

Dialling codes: Australia 0011 • Canada 011
New Zealand 00 • South Africa 09 • UK 00 • USA 011

Telephoning from the Czech Republic

00 + country code + local number

Dialling Codes: Australia 61 • Canada 1
New Zealand 64 • South Africa 27 • UK 44 • USA 1

International operator: 1181

+420 ... ...

Prague, the most popular tourist destination in the Czech Republic, is visited annually by more than two million foreigners (most of them from Great Britain, France, Germany and the USA)

COMMUNICATIONS

POST

Post offices around Prague's centre are open on weekdays from 8 am to 6 pm. The main post office at Jindřišská 14 (close to the metro station Můstek) is open daily from 7 am to 8 pm. In order to be served, you must use the Q-matic machine, located at the door to the huge entrance hall. If you're buying stamps it's wise to buy a few at a time. The minimum price for sending a letter is 17 CZK for EU destinations and 18 CZK for all other destinations.

INTERNET

Internet cafes with high speed internet access dot the city centre and offer good rates. Most are open on weekends.

PUBLIC PHONES

Public telephones are either coin- or card--operated. You can buy telephone cards at post offices, newsagents and kiosks or tobacconists. For international calls, you can buy a pre-paid card at the above-mentioned places; this option costs significantly less than calling using coins.

MOBILE PHONES

Almost everyone has a mobile phone using the major mobile networks O2, Vodafone and T-Mobile. If you decide to bring your mobile phone from home, make sure you enable your roaming programme so that you can receive calls once you're in Prague. Prague uses GSM 900/1800. T: +420/220 400 611

 +420 ... ...

Foreigners' Police in Prague:

Olšanská 2, 130 00 Prague 3

T: 420/974 820 229, cppkr@mvcr.cz

EMBASSIES

- GREAT BRITAIN

Thunovská 14, Prague 1, 118 00

T: 420/257 402 111, www.britain.cz

"A" Malostranská

- USA:

Tržiště 15, Prague 1, 118 00

T: 420/257 530 663, www.usembassy.cz

"A" Malostranská

- CANADA

Muchova 6, Prague 6, 160 00

T: 420/272 101 800, www.canada.cz

"A" Hradčanská

- AUSTRALIA

Klimentská 1207/10, Prague 1

T: 420/296 578 350

"B" Náměstí Republiky

- SOUTH AFRICA

Ruská 65, Prague 10 - Vršovice

T: 420/267 311 114

"A" Skalka — "138" Tolstého

- JAPAN

Maltézské nám. 6, Prague 1, 118 01

T: 420/257 533 546, www.cz.emb-japan.go.jp

"A" Malostranská

NETHERLANDS

Gotthardská 6/27, Prague 6–Bubeneč

www.netherlandsembassy.cz

T: 420/233 015 200

"A" Hradčanská – "131" Sibiřské n.

GENERAL OPENING HOURS:

- State Offices:

Mon–Fri: 8.00–12.00 and 13.00–15.00 (on Mon and Wed till 17.00), closed Sat and Sun.

- Embassies:

Mon–Thu: 8.30–16.00, Fri: 8.30–15.00.

Submit visa applications in the mornings.

Closed Sat and Sun.

The tourist season is from 1 April to 31 October

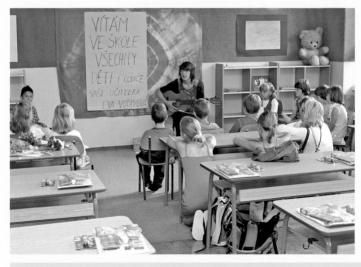

The school year starts 1 September and ends 30 June

- Banks: Mo–Fri: 9.00–17.00, closed on Sat and Sun.
- Shops – grocery stores: 7.00 –18.00, Sat 7.00–12.00, closed Sun. Supermarkets and hypermarkets are open every day, some with 24 hour service.
- Pharmacies: Mon–Fri: 8.00–18.00, Sat and Sun closed.

Pharmacies with non-stop service in Prague:
Letná, Fr. Křižíka 22, Prague 7
U Anděla, Štefánikova 6/250, Prague 5
Palackého 720/5, Nové Město, Prague 1

- Museums, galleries:
Tue–Sun: 9.00–18.00. Many are closed on Mondays, with the exception of July and August.
- Monuments, sights, castles and chateaux:
Tue–Sun: 9.00–15.00 (season 9.00–18.00) The last tour usually starts an hour before closing time. Many castles and chateaux are closed in the winter months.
- Admission to sights:
Expect to pay between 20 CZK to 200 CZK. Some galleries and museums accept international discount cards: GO 25, ISIC,

ITIC and Euro 26. Larger tourist groups and families also may receive a discount.

THE SCHOOL YEAR

The school year starts on September 1st and finishes on June 30th.

- Summer school holidays are in summer (July, August).
- Winter break is during the Christmas period (around two weeks)
- Spring Break varies from region to region, but is commonly a week between February and March.

Please note: Public transport schedules change during school break.

THE TOURIST SEASON

As a rule, the tourist season begins April 1st and ends October 31st. During this period most monuments are open. Outside the season (with the exception of the Christmas and New Years' holidays) accommodation and some tourist services tend to be cheaper.

▼ (km) ▶ PRAHA

Amsterdam	891	Dublin	1820	Luxembourg	731	Sofiya	1281	Brno	200
Athína	1946	Genève	919	Madrid	2300	Stockholm	1541	České Budějovice	150
Belfast	2045	Helsinki	2178	Minsk	1149	Tallin	1562	Hradec Králové	115
Beograd	904	Istanbul	1836	Moskva	1855	Tiranë	1422	Karlovy Vary	130
Berlin	341	København	927	Paris	1031	Valencia	2048	Liberec	100
Bratislava	328	Kyjiv	1389	Rїga	1260	Vilnius	1042	Plzeň	95
Brussel	902	Lisboa	2814	Roma	1281	Warszawa	612	Olomouc	280
Bucureşti	1304	Ljubljana	664	Sarajevo	1046	Wien	285	Ostrava	380
Budapest	522	London	1272	Skopje	1324	Zagreb	645	Ústí nad Labem	95

MOTORWAY PERMITS /2007/		
	up to 3.5 t	3,5 t – 12 t
1 year	1 000 CZK	8,000 CZK
1 month	330 CZK	2,000 CZK
1 week	220 CZK	750 CZK

ROAD TRANSPORT IN THE CZECH REPUBLIC

712 km of road are toll roads, of which 500 km are motorway and the remainder high-speed roads (D1, D2, D3, D5, D8, D11, 47).

- Motorway permits: several types are on sale, they apply to cars and trucks
- The highest permitted speeds in the Czech Republic: built-up areas 50 km/h, outside urban areas 90 km/h, motorways 130 km/h
- Lights: you must drive at all times with your headlights on

- Border Crossings:

Germany: Varnsdorf, Hřensko, Cínovec, Boží Dar, Aš, Rozvadov, Folmava, Železná Ruda

Austria: Dolní Dvořiště, Slavonice, Mikulov, Poštorná

Poland: Český Těšín, Bohumín, Krnov, Náchod

Slovakia: Mosty u Jablunkova, Horní Bečva, Střelná, Brumov-Bylnice, Starý Hrozenkov, Strání, Hodonín, Břeclav, Lanžhot

- Import–export: EU regulations apply. Tax-free limits for selected goods: 800 cigarettes, 10 litres of spirits, 90 litres of wine, 110 litres of beer, 1 kg of tobacco

MONEY, EXCHANGE OFFICE:

- Currency: Czech Crown 1 CZK, 100 heller
- Coins: 1 CZK, 2 CZK, 5 CZK, 10 CZK, 20 CZK, 50 CZK
- Banknotes: 50 CZK, 100 CZK, 200 CZK, 500 CZK, 1 000 CZK, 2 000 CZK, 5 000 CZK
- Exchange: you can change money in the bank, at the Post Office and in Exchange Offices.
- A word to the wise: In exchange offices, the sale exchange of the currencies is often displayed *we sell*. This is confusing, as the rate they will buy your foreign notes is different. Ask about the transaction charges, before you commit.

Don´t change money in the street!

Swindlers will offer you a better rate, but you may end up either with forged banknotes or banknotes from another country (most often Bulgarian Leva).

ATMs, or automatic teller machines, are on almost every street corner in the centre of Prague.

Credit and debit cards are accepted in most places – most often VISA, MasterCard a AmEx. It is becoming more and more common to pay in Euro.

80

The face sides of banknotes have portraits of famous personalities from Czech history:

20 CZK – <u>Přemysl Otakar I</u> *(1155/?/–1230)*
In 1198 this ruler of the Premysl family received his inherited King's title. In 1212 the rights of the Bohemian Kingdom were confirmed (the Golden Bull of Sicily).
This banknote has been withdrawn from circulation and is no longer legal tender!

50 CZK – <u>St. Agnes of Bohemia</u> *(1211–1282)*
She was a Přemysl family princess who was canonized in 1989. She founded cloisters and devoted herself to charity. She is the founder of the sole Bohemian order of knights – Crusaders of the Red Star.

100 CZK – <u>Charles IV of Luxembourg</u> *(1316–1378)*
He was King of Bohemia and Germany and from 1355 Emperor of the Holy Roman Empire. A prominent and active European ruler in the late Middle Ages.

200 CZK – <u>Jan Amos Komenský</u> *(1592–1670)*
Thinker, pedagogue, theologian, writer and historian. In 1628, he had to emigrate from the country.

500 CZK – <u>Božena Němcová</u> *(1820–1862)*
She is considered to be the most prominent Bohemian writer. She is the author of small prose works with patriotic and social themes.

1 000 CZK – <u>František Palacký</u> *(1798–1876)*
Scientist and historian – he recorded the national history. An important figure in Bohemian cultural and political life.

2 000 CZK – <u>Ema Destinnová</u> *(1878–1930)*
An opera singer who sang in Berlin and the Metropolitan Opera in New York.

5 000 CZK – <u>Tomáš Garrigue Masaryk</u> *(1850–1937)*
The founder and first president of independent Czechoslovakia (from 1918). Philosopher, statesman, and sociologist.

PRAGUE AT A GLANCE

- <u>Area:</u> 496 km^2
- <u>Number of inhabitants:</u> 1,178,600
- <u>Geographical situation:</u>
latitude 50.05 N; longitude 14.22 E
- <u>Average height above sea-level:</u> 230 m
- <u>River:</u> a stretch of 30 km of the Vltava runs through the city, maximum width 330 m, with nine islands along the edge of the city
- <u>Administrative division of the city:</u>
22 administrative districts, 57 municipal parts
- <u>Historic districts:</u> Hradčany (Castle Quarter), Mála Strana (Lesser Town), Staré Město (Old Town), Josefov (Jewish Quarter), Nové Město (New Town), Vyšehrad

The U Fleků Brewery
is probably the most famous Prague restaurant, dating from the 15th century. It now houses a Brewery Museum.

SOME PRAGUE SUPERLATIVES

- <u>The oldest preserved fountain:</u> the singing fountain (1568) in the Royal Garden
- <u>The oldest café</u> – Slávia (opened in 1881)
- <u>The oldest meteorological observatory:</u> – Klementinum (meteorological observations since 1752)
- <u>The oldest bridge:</u> Charles Bridge (1357)
- <u>The oldest railway station:</u> Masaryk (1845)
- <u>The oldest hospital:</u> Na Františku (1354)
- <u>The oldest brewery:</u> U Fleků (founded in 1499)
- <u>The oldest rotunda:</u> St. Martin´s in Vyšehrad (11th century)
- <u>The oldest pipe organ:</u> Týn Cathedral (1673)
- <u>The longest bridge:</u> Negrelli Viaduct (1 110 m)
- <u>The longest street:</u> Strakonická (15.5 km)
- <u>The deepest underground/subway station:</u> Náměstí míru (53 m deep)
- <u>The longest stretch of underground/subway between stations:</u> 2,749 m (Holešovice Station - Kobylisy, line C)
- <u>The shortest street:</u> Jiřího Červeného, at Kampa (measures 27 m)
- <u>The lowest point:</u> 172 m above sea-level (at the place where the Vltava leaves the borders of Prague – on the riverbed)
- <u>The biggest square in Prague and Czech Republic:</u> Karlovo náměstí (80,500 m^2)
- <u>The biggest swimming pool:</u> Podolský Swimming Stadium
- <u>The biggest stadium:</u> Strahov Stadium (area 310.5×202.5 m)
- <u>The biggest bell:</u> Zikmund (St. Vitus Cathedral, diameter 256 cm, height 203 cm, 16,500 kg)
- <u>The highest building:</u> the former Czech Radio building in Pankrác (height 109 m, 30 floors)
- <u>The highest bridge:</u> Nuselský Bridge (length 485 m, width 26 m, height 40 m)
- <u>The highest construction:</u> Žižkov Television Tower (216 m)
- <u>The highest point:</u> 399 m above sea-level, Teleček hill, Prague 5

The most well-known Prague café

Café Slávia on Národní Street, opposite the Národní Divadlo (National Theatre) is probably the most well-known Prague café. From the 19th century until now, this café has been a meeting place for distinguished personalities from Czech's cultural scene.

TRANSPORT IN PRAGUE:

- Single Tickets:

Adults (+ children older than 15 years)

transferable: 26 CZK, non-transferable: 18 CZK

Children from 6 to 15 years, and large pieces of luggage transferable: 13 CZK,

non-transferable: 9 CZK

Please note: Remember to frank your tickets in the yellow boxes with arrows found on trams and buses and the entrance to underground metro stations

- Non-transferable tickets are valid for buses and trams for a maximum of 20 minutes for a single journey. They are valid for a maximum of 4 stops on the underground/subway and you can change lines. These tickets are valid for a maximum of 30 minutes. From 20.00 until 5.00 and at the weekends they are valid for 30 minutes.

- Transferable tickets are valid for 75 minutes on every type of public transport (bus, tram, underground/subway, cable car). These tickets are valid for 90 minutes between 20.00–5.00 and at weekends.

- Transportation zones: Prague is divided into five zones. A standard two-zone ticket suffices for movement within the area of the capital city.

A WORD TO THE WISE: Don't ride in the black. There are metro controllers everywhere in Prague, and they level a hefty fine to anyone riding without a properly franked ticket. Fines start at 500 CZK. To make matters worse, there are people dressed as metro controllers, lurking around stations for the unwary traveller. Do not hand over your passport in any situation, and the metro controller must show you a golden badge with the public transport logo on it, and give you a receipt for your fine. Once you've paid the fine, you can ride public transport free for the next hour.

PUBLIC TRANSPORT PASSES:

- one day for all zones: 100 CZK, reduced 50 CZK
- 3-day: 330 CZK
- 5-day: 500 CZK
- 30-day: 670 CZK
- 90-day: 1,880 CZK

When visiting Prague it is better to leave the car outside the centre and to use public transport

Lost and found:

Karolíny Světlé 5, Prague 1, 110 00

T: +420/224 235 085

UNDERGOUND/SUBWAY

A: green (Dejvická–Depo Hostivař)

B: yellow (Zličín- Černý most)

important stops: Florenc (the main bus station), Anděl (bus station), Smíchovské nádraží (railway station).

The ticket is valid on all types of public transport in Prague – travellers are required to frank their tickets immediately on entering the vehicle. This is a transfer ticket that costs CZK 26.
(See page 83)

C: red (Háje–Letňany)

important stops: Hlavní nádraží (the main railway station), Vyšehrad, Nádraží Holešovice (railway station), Roztyly (bus station), Florenc (the main bus station)

Operates daily, 5.00 until 24.00.

TRAMS

numbers 1 to 26 operate during the day

night service: 9 lines from nr. 51 to 59

The central point for night time tram service is at Lazarská stop.

Operate daily, 4.30 until 24.00.

Night service at 30 minute intervals from 0.30 till 4.30.

BUSES

180 routes daily and 16 night routes numbered from 502–514 and 601–603.

Daily service, 4.30 until 24.00.

Night time service at intervals of 30 minutes from 0.30 until 4.30.

TAXI

– Order taxis via a non-stop dispatching service and find out the cost of your ride beforehand

– Only choose the kind of taxi service vehicles that are equipped with a securely attached roof light with TAXI written on it and that are marked with a registration number, company name, price list with a basic rate, rate per kilometre, and the rate for one minute of waiting

– Make sure the car has a taxi-fare meter and that it is turned on

– After you reach your destination always ask for a receipt printed on the printer of the taxi-fare meter, which should also include the kilometres and price.

- Every company has its own rates. The maximum prices are:

25 CZK per 1 km for trips within Prague,

A one-off fee of 34 CZK for getting in the taxi,

5 CZK per 1 minute for waiting. Prices may increase during the year. Prices for trips outside of Prague are not limited.

Tram

- Taxi services:

AAA radiotaxi, tel.: +420/222 333 222

Profi -Taxi, tel.: +420/844 700 800

Taxi Praha, tel.: +420/222 111 000

Citytaxi, tel.: +420/257 257 257

Taxi Sedop, tel.: +420/271 722 222

Halotaxi, tel.: +420/244 114 411

- Modrý anděl (Blue angel)

– Driving your car for you:

+420/272 700 202

P

PARK AND RIDE, CAR PARKS

It is better for visitors to Prague to leave their cars at designated park and ride stops, indicated by the P+R sign, and to continue by public transport. The park and ride car parks are located along underground/subway lines: line A (Skalka); line B (Zličín, Nové Butovice, Palmovka, Rajská zahrada, Černý most); line C (Nádraží Holešovické, Opatovice).

In the city centre, there are multi-storey car parks and guarded car parks. Paid parking in the centre is divided into three zones: Orange – max. 2 hours; green – max. 6 hours (both zones have parking ticket machines); blue – only for residents and local companies dispaying a parking pass. Please note: ilegally parked cars will be clamped or towed away. Do not leave valuable items visible in cars outside guarded parking areas.

22 – DAILY SERVICE (4.30–24.00) 54 – NIGHT TIME SERVICE (0.30–4.30)	▼M	🚋	🚌	
PRAGUE CASTLE (PRAŽSKÝ HRAD)	A – MALOSTRANSKÁ	22, 23 – PRAŽSKÝ HRAD		
	A – HRADČANSKÁ	22, 23 – POHOŘELEC		
		1, 8 – HRADČANSKÁ		
		12, 18 – MALOSTRANSKÁ		
WENCESLAS SQUARE (VÁCLAVSKÉ NÁMĚSTÍ)	A, C – MUZEUM	3, 9, 14, 24 VÁCLAVSKÉ NÁMĚSTÍ		
	A, B – MŮSTEK			
		54, 55, 56, 58 VÁCLAVSKÉ NÁMĚSTÍ		
MAIN RAILWAY STATION	C – HLAVNÍ NÁDRAŽÍ	5, 9, 26 HLAVNÍ NÁDRAŽÍ	504, 505, 509, 511, 513 HLAVNÍ NÁDRAŽÍ	
MAIN BUS STATION	A, C – FLORENC	8, 24 – SOKOLOVSKÁ	207, 133, 135 – FLORENC	
		52 – SOKOLOVSKÁ		
CHARLES BRIDGE	A – STAROMĚSTSKÁ	17, 18 NOVOTNÉHO LÁVKA		
		53 – NOVOTNÉHO LÁVKA		

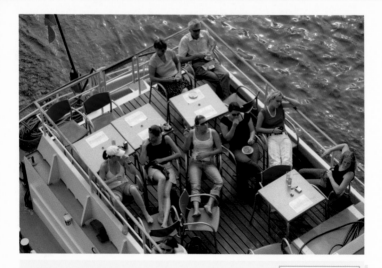

Boat transport in Prague

gives you a unique view of the town centre and a pleasant, romantic trip along the Vltava, seeing many tourist attractions on the way. The EVD Company offers daily one-hour boat trips from 10.00 to 18.00, two-hour excursions from 15.00–17.00, a lunch and music cruise from noon – 14.00 and a dinner and music cruise from 19:00–22:00.
Embark next to the Čechův Bridge.
evd@paroplavba.cz; tel.: +420/224 810 030, +420/724 202 505, fax: +420/224 810 003

SIGHTSEEING TOURS OF PRAGUE AND ITS ENVIRONS

Visitors to Prague can make use of various offers of travel agencies for excursions around Prague. Tours with local, English-speaking tourist guides are provided by the «PREMIANT CITY TOUR» company. Reservations: +420/224 946 922, NONSTOP: +420/606 600 123, E-mail: info@premiant.cz

Selected Prague museums and galleries:

THE NATIONAL MUSEUM

Wenceslas Square 68, 115 79 Prague 1
▪ The Natural Science Museum
Departments: rocks and mineral; fossils, fungi, plants; insects; animals; human history; chemical research laboratory; wood dating laboratory
▪ Museum of History

Departments: Classical Archaeology, Early Czech History, Ethnic Studies, Modern Czech History, National Museum Archive, Numismatics, Physical Education and Sport, Pre- and Proto-history, Theatre
Permanent exhibitions:
The Prehistory of Bohemia, Moravia and Silesia
(main building of the National Museum)
Monuments of the National Past (Prague Castle – Lobkowitz Palace)
Monuments of Stone Sculpture in Bohemia
11th–19th century (Lapidárium – Výstaviště 422, Exhibition area, Prague 7);
Pharmaceutical culture and a view of Bohemian pharmacies from the Renaissance until the 19th Century (Nerudova Str. 32, Prague 1)
▪ Library of the National Museum
Sections: basic library; manuscripts and old prints;

book culture; services; international publication exchange; the Chateau Library; magazines

- <u>Náprstkovo Museum of Asian, African and American Culture</u>

Old Town, Betlémské náměstí 1, Prague 1

Asian Culture, Náprstkovo Museum Library, Near-East and Africa, Non-European Ethnography, Non-European Numismatics, Prehistory and Ancient History

- <u>Czech Museum of Music</u>

Novotného lávka 1, Prague 1

Departments: Musical History; Musical Instruments; Bedřich Smetana Museum; Antonín Dvořák Museum

Permanent exhibition:

Museum of Musical Instruments (Karmelitská 2/4); Bedřich Smetana Museum; Antonín Dvořák Museum (Villa America, Ke Karlovu 20, Prague 2); Antonín Dvořák Memorial; Smetana Jabkenice Lodge; Josef Suk Memorial Křečovice; Jaroslav Ježek Memorial (the Blue Room, Kaprova 10, Prague 2)

MUSEUM OF THE CAPITAL CITY OF PRAGUE

- <u>main building</u> ("B" Florenc)

Na Poříčí 52; Prague 8,

www.muzeumprahy.cz

<u>Permanent exhibition:</u> Historic Prague. History of the town and its inhabitants from prehistory until 1784; A unique model of Prague by Langweil from the years 1826–1834

- <u>Villa Müller, the work of the architect Adolf Loos</u>

Prague 6 – Střešovice

Nad Hradním vodojemem 14/642;

must book in advance. Tel. +420/224 312 012

- <u>Podskalská customs office in Výtoň</u>

Rašínovo nábřeží 412, 120 00 Prague 2

Exposition: Vanished Podskalí – Rafts and Ships on the Vltava

OTHER PRAGUE MUSEUMS

- <u>National Technical Museum</u>

Kostelní 42, Prague 7;

Acoustics; astronomy; film and photography; measurement of time; metallurgy; mining; telecommunications; railway transport hall (Masaryk Station)

- <u>Prague Jewellery Cabinet</u>

Hergetova Brickyard, Cihelna 2, Prague 1;

www.cihelna.info

Permanent exhibition: Jewels and Luxurious Decorations from the 17th Century till the Present. Collections of the Museum of Industrial Art in Prague

- <u>Franz Kafka Museum</u>

Hergetova cihelna, Cihelná 2, Prague 1;

("B" Malostranská)

www.kafkamuseum.cz

The world of famous Prague native, Franz Kafka. Audiovisual programmes, first editions of Kafka's works, photography, manuscripts, drawings and three-dimensional exhibits.

- <u>Mucha Museum</u>

Panská 7, Prague 1; www.mucha.cz

Unique collection of art nouveau works by Alfons Mucha.

A walk in the centre of the city

- Bertramka

The W. A. Mozart and Mr and Mrs Dušek Museum;
permanent exhibition: Personal mementos, musical
instruments, period engravings, pictures and
documents recording Mozart´s visits to Betramka
and Prague

("B" Anděl)

Mozartova 169, Prague 5

- Franz Kafka Exhibition

Náměstí Fr. Kafky 10, Prague 1

- Kampa Museum

František Kupka; Otto Gutfreund; Modern
Central European Art;

U Sovových mlýnů 503/2, Prague 1

- Museum of Childrens´Drawings

U Radnice 13, Prague 1 – Staré Město, dům U Zelené
žáby (House at the Green Frog)

- Museum of Communism

Exhibition: Prague and Czechoslovakia during
the Communist Era;

Na Příkopě 10, Prague 1

- Miniatures Museum

Strahovské nádvoří 11, Prague 1 (the Strahov
Monastery complex)

- Police Museum

Ke Karlovu 1, Prague 2

History, origin, development and activity of the
Czech security service, criminology and well-known
criminal cases, air services, the foreigners' and
border police, the former state security service.

- National Agricultural Museum

Kostelní 44, Prague 7

Food production in the 19th and 20th centuries, old
craft tools and workshop equipment.

- Museum of National Literature

Strahovské nádvoří 1, Prague 1

- J.A. Comenius Pedagogical Museum in Prague

Malá Strana (Lesser Town), Valdštejnská 20

J. A. Comenius and the Czech School. Collection
of old school books and educational aids, a 19th
century classroom.

- U Fleků Brewery Museum

Křemencova 11, Prague 1

- Postal Museum

Nové mlýny 2, Prague 1

- Family Postcard Museum

Liliová 4, Prague 1 – dům U Červené židle

Bertramka – Now a museum, it was here that W. A. Mozart composed Don Giovanni

(The House at the Red Chair); More than a thousand historic postcards from 1890–1930

- **Wax Figures Museum**

Two locations: Melantrichova 5, Prague 1; Mostecká 18, Prague 1

Czech and world personalities from the areas of culture, science and sport, Kaleidoscope Cinema highlighting famous historical Czechs

- **THE JEWISH MUSEUM IN PRAGUE**

U Staré školy 1, 3, Prague 1

www.jewishmuseum.cz/en

Maisel Synagogue

History of the Jews in Bohemia and Moravia from the 10th to the18th century;

Maiselova 10, Prague 1

Spanish Synagogue

The History of the Jews in Bohemia and Moravia – from emancipation till the present

Dušní, Prague 1

Winter Synagogue

house of prayer (1st floor) – exhibitions

Vězeňská 1, Prague 1

Pinkas Synagogue

Memorial to the holocaust victims from Czech and Moravia

Široká 3, Prague 1

Klausen Synagogue

Jewish traditions and customs

U Starého hřbitova 3a, Prague 1

Ceremonial Hall

Jewish traditions and customs

U Starého hřbitova 3a, Prague 1

Old Jewish Cemetery

entrance only from Široká 3, Prague 1

Education and Culture Centre

Reading room and research room

U Staré Školy (At the Old School) 1, 3, Prague 1

The Jewish Cemetery in Žižkov

Fibichova, Prague 3

The Spanish Synagogue

LEADING GALLERIES

- **THE NATIONAL GALLERY IN PRAGUE**

Staroměstské nám. 12, Prague 1

KINSKÝ PALACE

Housing a collection of drawings and graphic works

Staroměstské nám. 12, Prague 1

ŠTERNBERSKÝ PALACE

permanent exhibition: Epochs and personalities – European Art from Antiquity until the End of the Baroque.

Hradčanské nám. 15, Prague 1

THE MONASTERY OF ST. GEORGE

Art in Bohemia from the time from Emperor Rudolf II's court to the 19th century

Jiřské nám. 33, Prague 1 – Castle

THE MONASTERY OF ST. AGNES OF BOHEMIA

Medieval art in Bohemia and central Europe from 1200 to1550

U Milosrdných 17, Prague 1

ZBRASLAV CHATEAU – Asian art

Zbraslav, Prague 5

("B" Smíchovské nádraží – BUS "129, 241, 314, 318" Zbraslav)

VELETRŽNÍ PALACE

19th, 20th and 21st century art

Dukelských hrdinů 47, Prague 7

("C" Vltavská)

- <u>CZECH MUSEUM OF VISUAL AND GRAPHIC
ARTS:</u>
– modern art;
Husova Street , Prague 1
- <u>GALLERY OF THE CAPITAL CITY OF PRAGUE</u>
All expositions and exhibitions are closed on
Mondays.
U ZLATÉHO PRSTENU (HOUSE AT THE GOLD RING),
20th century Czech Art
Týnská 6, Prague 1 - Ungelt
ZÁMEK TROJA (CASTLE TROJA)
19th Century Czech Art
U Trojského zámku 1, Prague 7
(⧦ "C" Nádraží Holešovice – BUS "112" ZOO
Troja)
BÍLKOVA VILLA
František Bílek Studio
Mickiewiczova 1, Prague 6 - Hradčany

Exhibitions:
HOUSE AT THE BLACK MOTHER OF GOD
– Czech Cubism
Celetná 34, Prague 1
MUCHA MUSEUM
Exhibit of works by Alfons Mucha
Panská 7, Prague 1

PRAGUE MUSEUM OF INDUSTRIAL ART
The Story of Materials
17. listopadu 2, Prague 1

YEARLY CULTURAL EVENTS
- FEBIOFEST – international review of films, television and videos /January/
- PRAGUE SPRING – festival of classical music /January/
- SLOVAK THEATRE IN PRAGUE – Slovak theatre /February/
- EUROPEAN FILM DAYS – festival of contemporary European films /March/
- EUROPEAN FESTIVAL COMPETITION OF ACCORDION ORCHESTRAS /March/
- INTERFESTIVAL OF MAGIC – international festival of magic arts /March/
- AGHARTA PRAGUE JAZZ FESTIVAL
leading jazz personalities and orchestras /March– December/
- PRAGUE FESTIVAL OF AUTHORS – international meeting of literary authors /April/
- MUSICA ECUMENICA – festival of classical music /April/
- ONE WORLD – international human rights film festival /April/

Prague Spring International Music Festival
"Pražské jaro"

www.festival.cz/en

– is a constant parade of excellent artists, symphony orchestras and chamber groups. Since 1946, a host of personalities such as Ančerl, Bernstein, Sir A. Boult, Firkušný, Krombholc, Kubelík, Lympany, Mravinsky, Munch, Neveu, Novotná, Oborin, Oistrach, Panenka and others have performed. Since 1952 the festival has opened with the cycle of symphonic poems My Country by Bedřich Smetana and has closed with Ludwig van Beethoven´s 9th Symphony. The Prague Spring International Music Festival is one of the few world-class festivals to cultivate young performers.

- PRAGUE WORLD OF BOOKS – international book fair /May/
- PRAGUE SPRING – international music festival /May/
- KHAMORO – international festival of Roma culture /May/
- GOLDEN PRAGUE – international television festival of music and dance programmes /May/
- INTERNATIONAL CHOIR FESTIVAL OF FOLK SONGS /May/
- WORLD FESTIVAL OF PUPPETEERING /May–June/
- FESTPOL – FESTIVAL OF POLICE ORCHESTRAS AND CHOIRS /June/
- DANCE PRAGUE – international contemporary dance and theatre movement festival /June/
- MUSICA SACRA PRAGA – festival of sacral choirs /June/
- RESPECT – festival of ethnic and world music /June/
- SUMMER CELEBRATION OF OLD MUSIC international music festival /June–July/
- ETHNIC FESTIVAL – the biggest review of folk arts /June to September/
- ORGAN SUMMER – international festival of organ concerts /July to August/
- OPEN-AIR OPERA FESTIVAL in the courtyard of the Lichtenstein Palace /July to August/
- SUMMER SHAKESPEARE FESTIVAL – Open-air Shakespeare /July to September/
- INTERNATIONAL ORGAN FESTIVAL – organ concerts /August/

91

- INTERNATIONAL FESTIVAL OF STRING QUARTETS
festival in honour of Antonín Dvořák /Aug to Sept/
- YOUNG PRAGUE – international music festival
/August to September/

DISTINGUISHED PERSONALITIES WITH A CONNECTION TO PRAGUE

Aostalli, de Sala Ulrico (1525–1597) – Renaissance builder and architect of Prague Castle

Appollinaire, Guillaume (1880–1918) – poet; his visit to Prague inspired him to write "A Prague Walker"

from Arras, Matyáš (1290–1352) – builder and architect; started construction of St. Vitus Cathedral

Barrande, Joachim (1799–1883) – geologist and palaeontologist; the Barrandov Quarter is named after him

Beethoven, Ludwig van (1770–1827) – composer; he staged a number of public performances in 1796 in Prague

Bolzano, Bernard (1781–1848) – mathematician and philosopher, the forerunner of modern logic

Brahe, Tycho (1546–1601) – astronomer; active at the court of Rudolf II; buried in Týn Cathedral

Braun, Matyáš Bernard (1684–1738) – sculptor; creator of the statues on Charles Bridge (e.g. St. Luitgard)

Brod, Max (1884–1968) – author; published the writings of Franz Kafka

Brokoff, Ferdinand Maxmilián (1688–1731) – sculptor; author of statues on Charles Bridge

Tchaikovsky, Peter Ilyich (1840–1893) – composer; conducted his work on several visits to Prague

Čapek, Karel (1890–1938) – famous Czech author; works include The White Illness, Mother

Master Jan Hus
He is one of the most striking figures in Czech history. The Bohemian thinker and reformer of the Church was labelled a heretic for his opinions and in 1415 was burned at the stake by the Council of Constance. Even while at the stake, he did not recant his teachings. Hus's death was one of the impetuses for beginning the Hussite revolution, which affected not only Bohemia but a large part of Europe. The picture shows the Master Jan Hus monument on Old Town Square by artist Ladislav Šaloun (1915)

Dienzenhofer, Kilián Ignác (1689–1751) – baroque architect; works include Cathedral of St. Mikuláš

Dvořák, Antonín (1841–1904) – Czech composer, known for Slavonic Dances

Einstein, Albert (1879–1955) – physicist; professor at the German University in Prague (1911–1912)

Hašek, Jaroslav (1883–1923) – Czech author who wrote The Adventures of the good Soldier Švejk during World War I

Holar, Václav (1607–1677) – engraver and draughtsman; author of graphic sheets, drawn maps and portraits

Hus, Jan (around 1371–1415) – religious reformer; preacher in the Bethlehem Chapel (1402-1412)

Ibn Yaqub, Ibrahim († after 970) – Jewish trader and diplomat; first to include Prague in his chronicles

Kafka, Franz (1883–1924) – Czech-German author who wrote The Trial, The Castle, America

Kubelík, Rafael (1914–1996) – Czech conductor and composer for the Czech Philharmonic (1942–1948)

Liszt, Ferenc (1811–1886) – Hungarian composer, conductor and pianist; frequently gave concerts in Prague

Mahler, Gustav (1860–1911) – composer and conductor

Mozart, Wolfgang Amadeus (1756–1791) – composer; premiered the opera Don Giovanni in Prague in 1787

Mucha, Alfons (1860–1939) – painter; he became famous for his theatre posters during the Art Nouveau period.

Myslbek, Josef Václav (1848–1922) – sculptor; author of the St. Vaclav memorial on Wenceslas Square

Negrelli, Alois (1799–1858) – railway engineer and builder; creator of the unique Negrelli viaduct

Franz Kafka

Born in Prague in 1883, Kafka was a writer in the "Prague German literature" circle. Prague, the city in which he lived for most of his life inspired works such as The Trial, containing existential elements and set in mysterious, magical surroundings. Today, Prague and Kafka belong together, and that is why you will come across his likeness in many parts of Prague. (The statue in the photograph is by J. Róna and is on Dušní Street).

Nestroy, Johann Nepomuk (1801–1862) – dramatist; in the 1840s he staged his works in Prague

Parléř, Petr (1332–1399) – Late Gothic architect and sculptor; builder of St. Vitus Cathedral

Plečnik, Josip (1872–1957) – architect; carried out repairs to Prague Castle between 1920–1931

Rilke, Rainer Maria (1875–1926) – poet and author; Prague native

Seifert, Jaroslav (1901–1986) – poet; awarded the Nobel Prize for Literature

Šaljapin, Fjodor (1873–1938) – opera singer

Škréta, Karel (1610–1674) – baroque painter; decorated the Cathedral of St. Nicholas

de Vries, Adrian (around 1545–1626) – court sculptor to Rudolf II; made the statues for the Wallenstein Palace

Weber, Carl Maria von (1786–1826) – composer and conductor; director of the opera in the Stavovské Theatre

Werfel, Franz (1890–1945) – author; wrote Class Reunion, Forty Days of Musa Dagh

PRAGUE OVER THE CENTURIES

From 4000 BC – the oldest traces of prehistoric settlement around Prague

5th to 2nd centuries BC – Celtic hill fort and oppidum in Závisti u Zbraslavy (near Prague) was the centre of Celtic culture

9 BC – Marbod leads the Marcomanni into Bohemia (aristocratic seat in Bubeneč)

539 – Langobard King Wacho dies

5th–6th century – arrival of the Slavs

6th century – Slav culture of the Prague type with its centre in Roztoky u Prahy

8th century – the oldest settlement in the old Prague (a village in the Lesser Town)

8th–9th century – foundation of Prague Castle (there is evidence that it was a princely seat prior to

880 – the beginning of the rule of the Přemyslids)

926 – foundation of St. Vitus rotunda at Prague Castle

973 – foundation of Prague bishopric

11th century – building of stone Romanesque houses in Prague

1135–82 – Romanesque renovation of Prague Castle

1169 – construction works starts on the stone Judith bridge

1232–34 – Old Town acquires municipal rights and ramparts

1257 – New Town founded, later referred to as the Smaller and now Lesser Town

1310 – beginning of the reign of the Luxembourgs

1316 – last conflagration in the Old Town

1338 – Old Town obtains the right to have a town hall

1344 –Prague bishopric is elevated to an archbishopric; Gothic reconstruction of St. Vitus Cathedral commences

1348 – Charles IV founds Charles University and the New Town

1357 – work starts on the construction of a stone bridge (the Charles Bridge)

1402–13 – protestant reformer Jan Hus preaches in the Bethlehem Chapel

1419 – first defenestration of the aldermen and the start of the Hussite wars

1471 – beginning of the reign of the Jagiellonians

1483 – Second Prague defenestration of the aldermen and the onset of religious toleration

1486–1502 – the Late Gothic renovation of Prague Castle

1526 – beginning of the reign of the Habsburgs

1541 – fire in the Lesser Town, Hradčany and Prague Castle

1584–1612 – Prague is the residence of Emperor Rudoph II.

1618 – Third Prague defenestration and beginning of the thirty-years-war

1620 – Battle of the White Mountain and the defeat of the Uprising of the Estates

1648 –Swedes plunder the Rudolphine collections, Prague Castle and the Lesser Town

1784 – unification of the Prague towns into a single town of Prague

1787 – world premiere of *Don Giovanni* by Mozart

*On **August 20, 1968**, the military forces of the Warsaw Pact (Soviet Union, Poland, East Germany, Bulgaria, and Hungary) entered Czechoslovakia and ended the democratization process, culminating into events known as the Prague Spring.*

1818 – foundation of the National Museum

1848 – Slav Congress and revolution in Prague

1868 – festive ground breaking for the National Theatre

1891 – Jubilee Exhibition and the flowering of Art-Nouveau in Prague

1909–11 – construction of the Cubist House at the Black Mother of God

1918 – Proclamation of the Czechoslovak Republic

1939 – Hitler's occupation of Prague; Czechoslovakia becomes the Protectorate of Bohemia and Moravia

1945 – The May uprising and liberation of Prague

1948 – Communist military coup

1965 – breaking ground for the underground subway system (1974 came into service)

1968 – Warsaw Pact forces occupation of Czechoslovakia

1969 – student Jan Palach sets himself on fire in Prague to protest the occupation – two months later, student Jan Zajíc does the same

1989 – Velvet Revolution and the reintroduction of democracy

1993 – the division of Czechoslovakia into two separate countries: Czech and Slovak Republic; Prague is placed on the UNESCO list of monuments

1999 – Czech Republic enters NATO

2004 – Czech Republic joins the EU

2006 – The International Astronomical Union congress (IAU) took place in Prague

2009 – The Czech Republic's presidency of the EU Council

November 1989
– the "socialist" State power harshly suppressed a peaceful student demonstration. This action evoked a wave of demonstrations against the State system, which culminated in establishing democracy in society. Due to their peaceful nature, the events in November received the name "Velvet Revolution". On January 1, 1990, Václav Havel, a dissident of totalitarianism, became President.

Goulash with potato and bread dumplings

DINING OUT

- USEFUL DINING PHRASES

· I would like a table for . . . people.

Prosím, stůl pro . . . osob.

· Waiter/waitress!

Prosím Vás!

· May I have the bill, please?

Zaplatím, prosím.

· Could I have it well-cooked /medium/rare/, please?

Může to být hodně /středně/jen lehce/ propečené, prosím?

*A delicacy of Czech cuisine – **Svíčková na smetaně** – sirloin of beef in cream sauce with bread dumplings, garnished with cranberries*

· I am a vegetarian. Does this contain meat?

Jsem vegetarián. Není v tom maso?

· Where is the toilet (restroom) please?

Kde je záchod, prosím?

· I would like a cup of /two cups of/ coffee (tea).

Prosím šálek /dva šálky/ kávy (čaje).

more on pp. 108, 109

- BEST BITES:

Czech food is tasty and hearty, and not for dieters. The following items are most commonly found on a Czech restaurant menu, and are definitely worth a taste. Most of the Prague restaurants have an English menu, or the waiters speak English. Just ask, "Anglický prosím?" (English, please?) and see what happens. If you choose to eat in a pub rather than a tourist restaurant, you'll be hard-pressed to spend more than 15 Euro for your soup, main and drink.

Bramboračka – potato soup

Hemenex – ham and eggs

Omeleta – omelette

Svíčková na smetaně – cut of beef in an orange vegetable cream sauce with dumplings, usually garnished with a dollop of whipped cream and cranberry sauce

<u>Kapr</u> – Carp, from local fish-ponds, served "smažený" (fried) or "přírodní" (natural)

<u>Guláš</u> – Goulash, served with bread dumplings

<u>Smažený sýr</u> – Breaded and fried cheese

<u>Vepřová, knedlíky a zelí</u> (traditional roast pork with dumplings and sauerkraut),

<u>ovocné knedlíky</u> (fruit-filled dumplings with cream or special sweet cheese)

or <u>jablečný závin</u> (apple strudel).

■ TIPPING:

The expected tip for good service is between 5 and 10 per cent, but if you think service was bad or unfriendly, you can forget the tip.

■ FAST FOOD

You can find "rychlé občerstvení" (fast-food windows) on just about any street corner in Prague. Try a "párek v rohlíku" (hot dog with ketchup and/ or mustard) or a "langoš" (fried dough with garlic, cheese or cinnamon sugar on top).

■ CZECH BEER

Pivo (beer) is the secret to a happy life. Czechs must be a very happy people; as they are the world leaders in per capita beer consumption at 320 half- -litres a year per capita. The first written record of Bohemian beer production goes back to 1088, but the history of brewing beer is much older.

Served cool by the half-litre with a thick, frothy head, it must be cool, not cold. A proper pilsner takes seven minutes to pour. To feel at home in Prague, you need to learn just one simple phrase: "Ještě jedno pivo prosím" (One more beer, please).

• you most often come across draught beer which is popularly called "desítka" (ten) – it contains up to 4 % alcohol and also "lager" type beer called "dvanáctka" (twelve) which contains approximately 5.5 % alcohol. Occasionally, you will find special beers with higher alcohol content.

Sitting and relaxing on a terrace on Old Town Square

• most produced beers are light and clear and range from the bitter pilsner type to the light and slightly sweet bavarian type. The range is supplemented by dark beer; light and dark beer mixed together in the glass is called cut beer – popularly known as "řezaný".

A small snack with your beer?

<u>"Utopenec"</u> (Drowned man) – so-called because it consists of soft, strong, spicy sausage filled with onion and spicy paprika, seasoned with pepper and covered or "drowned" in a liquid made from water, vinegar and salt. After several days in cold storage, the smoked meat becomes a spicy delicacy.

<u>Pivní sýr</u> – a little cream is added to dairy cheese and it is whipped up into a froth into which a small amount of fresh garlic is pressed.

<u>Topinka</u> – This is a piece of dark bread fried in salt, garlic and lard or oil. It is traditionally served with scrambled eggs, grated cheese, meat mixture, or spicy cheese spread.

<u>Pickled Hermelin</u> – Hermelin is a camembert-type cheese. This one has been marinated in oil with onion, garlic, hot peppers and spices.

Beer *– "The golden vintage" – is the Czechs' favourite beverage and even evokes a feeling of national pride. Every Czech drinks on average 320 beers a year – leaving Czechs as the world leaders in per capita beer consumption. Beer has to be well-chilled (around 6–8 °C) and must have a strong flavour!*
Such as the "Pilsner" beer at U Pinkasů, not far from Wenceslas Square.

<u>Salty pastries</u> – various types of salty pastries are also usually available in our country to accompany beer. Pretzels are particularly popular.

- SELECTED RECIPES

<u>SIRLOIN OF BEEF IN CREAM SAUCE</u>

– is served with bread dumplings. It is an excellent dish based on larded beef which is baked or braised with a vegetable base. Afterwards this base is used in the preparation of a thicker cream sauce which is sweetened to taste. Sirloin of beef in cream sauce is decorated on the plate with a spoonful of cranberry sauce and a slice of lemon.

<u>GOULASH:</u>

You will need to prepare the following to feed four sturdy lads:

Pork (shoulder)	500 g
Pork liver	250 g
Pork kidneys	200 g
Onion	400 g
Pork lard	100 g
Minced sweet pepper	20 g
Salt	20 g
Garlic	50 g
Smooth flour	80 g

Marjoram, caraway, ground black pepper
Pork stock

Procedure:

• Cut the pork into smaller pieces, add salt, pepper and garlic, mix thoroughly and leave it to stand in its juices overnight.

• Sauté the evenly chopped onion in the lard. When it starts to change colour add cubes of home-made bacon. As soon as the onion browns, sprinkle it with sweet pepper and after briefly simmering it pour in the stock. Add the marinated meat, cumin and simmer with the lid on.

• When the meat is semi-soft add the small chopped pieces of cleaned kidneys and liver. Simmer everything and afterwards slightly thicken the mixture with béchamel (see below). It is also traditional to thicken the mixture with breadcrumbs.

• Finally flavour everything with ground dried marjoram or pepper. It is often the case at pig-killings that the boiled heart, tongue, spleen and the like are put into the goulash.

Béchamel – also referred to in Czech cuisine as "zásmažka" – is smooth flour combined under heat with fat or oil. It is either prepared in a light colour or in various darker shades, according to the duration of the frying of the flour in fat and with regard to the dish which is to be thickened with the béchamel.

VARIETIES OF GOULASH IN BOHEMIA:

• the most usual form is beef gulash made from shins

• goulash with peppers and tomatoes and beans is popular

• Znojmo goulash is made with sweet and sour pickled cucumbers

• pieces of various smoked meats are very often put into gulash

• during the mushroom-picking season, try goulash with freshly steamed mushrooms

• a traditional dish is potato goulash, prepared with onions, smoked meat and boiled potatoes – naturally combined with pepper sauce – and in some cases, further refined with cream

Roast duck delights every gourmet

ROAST PORK WITH STEWED SAUERKRAUT AND DUMPLINGS

– a very popular dish colloquially known as pork-dumpling-cabbage ("vepřo-knedlo-zelo"). Naturally roasted pork with salt, caraway and garlic served with potato or bread dumplings and stewed sauerkraut or sweet cabbage and fried onion. It has a sweet and sour taste.

Recipe for stewed sauerkraut and dumplings:

bread dumplings for ten people :

wholemeal flour...900 g

milk..400 ml

diced stale rolls ....250 g

yeast ....50 g

eggs 2

salt and a little sugar

• Put two pinches of sugar into tepid milk, salt, yeast and a third of the flour. Mix everything well and let it rise.

Czech buns

Don't miss roast knee with horseradish!

• After the yeast has risen add the eggs and the remaining flour and mix everything into a smooth non-sticky dough. Slightly coat the rolls – finally work the balls into the dough, cover and let rise. Afterwards mix the dough again, cut it into equal parts and roll out oblong dumplings.

• After leavening, boil them in salted water for 15–20 minutes. Turn them over several times while boiling. After removing the boiled dumplings from the water, it is necessary to prick them with a fork or skewer so that the boiling dough can exhale the bitterness and won´t go hard.

• You cut regular round slices from the roll with a knife or thread.

These light bread dumplings are the perfect accompaniment to sauces and gravies that go with meat in Bohemia.

STEWED SAUERKRAUT – 10 PORTIONS:

White sauerkraut	1 500 g
onion	200 g
rendered lard or fat	100 g
smooth flour	50 g
granular sugar	50 g
salt, cumin, water	

• Cut the sauerkraut into short pieces, add boiling water, add a little cumin and put it on to boil. Stir occasionally.

• Fry the finely chopped onion in lard, fat or oil. When it starts to brown, sprinkle it with flour, let it stand for a short while and afterwards take it off the heat.

• Add sugar to the half-stewed cabbage and mix it well with the onion mixture and simmer while constantly stirring until it is completely stewed.

• Salt according to taste or make it more sour or sweet.

CZECH BUNS

– on a tray in the oven

smooth flour	800 g
wholemeal flour	400 g
eggs	3 pcs
milk	500 g
yeast	40 g
sugar	200 g
vanilla sugar	25 g
butter or fat	200 g
oil	150 g
lemon peel from a single lemon	
salt	20 g

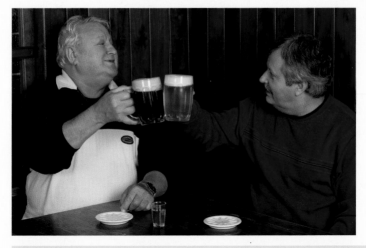

"Na zdraví!" (Cheers!)

poppyseed, cottage cheese and jam

filling of around .... 800 g

• Slightly heat the milk and mix the sugar, yeast, wholemeal flour and salt into it. Sprinkle on the smooth flour and leave it to rise in a covered casserole dish.

• Sprinkle sieved flour onto the leavened dough, add the eggs, lemon peel, vanilla sugar and the melted butter. Mix everything carefully and knead it into the smooth non-sticky dough. Then leave it to rise in a warm place.

• Mix the risen dough – stiffen it and spread it out on a pastry board with a rolling pin. At the same time, sprinkle flour on the dough. Then cut it into approx. 4 x 4 centimetre squares, put the filling in the middle of them and then seal them well and place them on the oiled tray and oil the individual scones where they touch the other ones.

• After rising bake them in the oven at medium temperature until golden.

• Remove cooled scones from the tray and sprinkle them with castor sugar.

■ PRAGUE SPECIALITY

<u>PRAGUE HAM</u> (pražská šunka)

This ranks amongst the typical delicacies of Prague cuisine. The ham is baked in bread dough. Unfortunately, you can only get this excellent starter in just few places. Don´t hesitate If you come across it.

"Utopenec" (Drowned man) /p. 97/

The most famous Czech football clubs are also great rivals

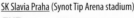

A 1st hockey league match

THE MOST POPULAR SPORTS

The most popular sports in the Czech Republic are football and ice-hockey. The highest-level competitions are played in Prague.

■ Football

Many famous Czech players play abroad for different leagues, such as Pavel Nedvěd, Petr Čech, Tomáš Rosický, and Milan Baroš.

The most popular clubs in Czech are the "Pražská S (Prague S)":

AC Sparta Praha (AXA Arena stadium, Prague-Letná)

"C" Vltavská – "1, 8, 25, 26" – Sparta

www.sparta.cz

SK Slavia Praha (Synot Tip Arena stadium)

"A" Flora – "136, 213" – „Slavia"

„6, 7, 22, 23, 24" – „Slavia"

www.slavia.cz

Season: VIII–XI, II–VI.

■ Hockey

The Sazka Arena is the most modern multi-purpose hall in the republic (built for the Ice-hockey World Championships in 2004). Famous Czech players play in the NHL and the CHL, such as Jaromír Jágr, Milan Hejduk, Patrik Eliáš and Martin Havlát. Two Prague teams play in the hockey extra league:

HC Sparta Praha (Tesla Arena)

"C" Nádraží Holešovice

www.hcsparta.cz

HC Slavia Praha (home games in the O2 Arena)

"B" Českomoravská

www.hc-slavia.cz

Season: IX–IV.

TIPS FOR EXCURSIONS

PRAGUE AND THE SURROUNDING AREA

■ Boat trips on the Vltava

Tourist boats depart from the riverbank near Čechův most (bridge) on sightseeing trips along the Vltava. (See page 86, Boat Transport in Prague)

■ Troja

The Baroque chateau of the same name is located

Prague Zoo

www.zoopraha.cz

in this district of Prague. **The Prague Botanic Gardens and Prague Zoo are nearby.**

 "C" Nádraží Holešovice – "112" – Zoologická zahrada

- <u>Smíchov</u>

A district on the left bank of the Vltava in front of the Lesser Town, the most visited attraction is the Villa Bertramka that hosted W. A. Mozart during his life, and hosts a a museum to the composer today. The Barrandov cliffs are nearby, where prehistoric fossils were discovered and the Barrandov film studios, where Czech films stars have been discovered since the 20th century.

CZECH REPUBLIC

- <u>Český Krumlov</u>

Located 150 km from Prague, in southern Bohemia, this impressive UNESCO town has a compact medieval core. The residence of the powerful House of Rožmberk until 1601, Český Krumlov's castle complex is the second largest in Czech Republic after Prague Castle, and its uniquely preserved Baroque Theatre is one of its many treasures.

www.ckrumlov.cz

www.visitceskykrumlov.cz

- <u>Karlovy Vary</u>

130 km south west of Prague, the most well-known and biggest spa town in our country has twelve hot springs, which are particularly therapeutic in the treatment of the digestive system. Its history reaches back to the 14th century, when Charles IV founded the town.

www. karlovyvary.cz

- <u>Olomouc</u>

270 km east of Prague, this lively university town and seat of the archbishopric was the centre of Moravian Margraves until the 17th century. Olomouc boasts the largest urban preservation area after Prague, and contains many architectural treasures, such as

Český Krumlov

Olomouc

the UNESCO-protected Baroque column of the Most Holy Trinity on its town square.

www.olomouc-tourism.cz

www.olomoucko.cz

- <u>Karlštejn</u>

20 km south west of Prague, this is probably the most popular and most visited castle in Bohemia today. Founded in 1348 by Charles IV, the crown jewels of the Holy Roman Empire are rumoured

to be hidden in the castle. The Gothic assemblage of 129 panelled paintings from the workshop of Master Theodoric in the Chapel of the Holy Cross is unique.

www.hradkarlstejn.cz

www.obeckarlstejn.cz

■ Kutná Hora

This town 70 km east of Prague is entered on the UNESCO list. The discovery of an extensive bed of silver here in the 13th century played an important role in its history as it became one of the richest towns in Europe over the next 300 years. The town's Gothic and Late Gothic monuments, such as the Cathedral of St. Barbora, are worthy of attention.

www. kutnahora.com

www.kh.cz

■ Lednice-Valtice complex

About 250 km south east of Prague, this large UNESCO protected area in South Moravia is formed by the artificial landscape surrounding the Lednice and Valtice chateaux and features a range of historical monuments until the 19th century when its English park was created.

www.radnice-valtice.cz

www.lednice.cz

■ Kroměříž

270 km east of Prague, this historic UNESCO town prides itself on its chateau complex and gardens that were once the archbishop's summer residence.

■ Mariánské Lázně

160 km west of Prague, this spa resort with mineral springs makes up the "spa triangle" with Karlovy Vary and Františkovy Lázně.

www.marianske-lazne.info

www.marianskelazne.cz

www.marianskelazne.com

■ Hluboká nad Vltavou

140 km south of Prague, this romantic Windsor-styled chateau ranks as one of the most attractive tourist destinations in our country.

www.visithluboka.cz ; www.hluboka.cz

Lednice

Karlštejn

■ Litomyšl

This town located 160 km east of Prague is known as the birthplace of Bedřich Smetana. Its UNESCO protected chateau is a typical example of central European Renaissance architecture with rich sgraffito decoration.

www.litomysl.cz

■ Třebíč

170 km south east of Prague, this sleepy town has a uniquely preserved and UNESCO protected Jewish quarter.

www.trebic.cz

■ Telč

150 km south east of Prague, the town's UNESCO protected Gothic and Renaissance buildings hearken back to the 16th century.

www.telc.cz

▪ Žďár nad Sázavou

150 km south east of Prague, the most valuable monument in the town is found on the summit of the Green Mountain – the UNESCO-protected Gothic Baroque pilgrimage church of St. John Nepomuk.

▪ Holašovice

140 km south of Prague, this tiny, South Bohemian UNESCO-protected hamlet pleases visitors with its "Peasant Baroque" farmsteads surrounding a small park and fish pond. www.holasovice.cz

▪ Brno

200 km south east of Prague, this is the second biggest city in the Czech Republic. The centre of Moravia, this modern city with a historic core features such UNESCO-listed gems as the early 20th century Functionalist Villa Tugendhat. www.brno.cz

▪ Ostrava

360 km east of Prague, the third largest city in Czech Republic is located in North Moravia. It boomed in the early 19th century in connection with coal mining. Today, Ostrava is a modern city with interesting industrial architectural monuments. Stodolní Street, with its many bars and pulsating night life is a popular attraction. www.ostravainfo.cz

▪ Příbram Mining Museum

The largest mining museum in the Czech Republic was founded in 1886 and presents the rich mining past of the Příbram region, linked with the mining of silver since medieval times. The tour includes a ride in two mining trains, riding in an elevator underground, and descending into a mine via a slide. Two historic steam mining machines and a large underground waterwheel are unique exhibits. The museum also presents mining folklore in a traditional miner's cottage and has a valuable mineralogical collection. www.muzeum-pribram.cz

Hluboká nad Vltavou

 Litomyšl

Příbram Mining Museum

National timetable information system: www.idos.cz

SHORT DICTIONARY

GREETINGS	
Good day	Dobrý den
Good bye	Na shledanou
Hi / Bye	Ahoj / Čau
Good morning	Dobré ráno
Good night	Dobrou noc

BASIC COMMUNICATIVE EXPRESSIONS	
Yes	Ano
No	Ne
Thank you	Děkuji
Please	Prosím
How are you?	Jak se máte?
Very well thank you.	Děkuji, dobře.
And you?	A vy?
Excuse me.	Promiňte.
Do you speak English?	Mluvíte anglicky?
I understand.	Rozumím.
I don´t understand.	Nerozumím.
Write it down for me, please.	Napište mi to, prosím.
Can you help me?	Můžete mi pomoci?
Wait a minute, please.	Počkejte, prosím.
Who?	Kdo?
What?	Co?
When?	Kdy?
What time is it?	Kolik je hodin?
Monday	Pondělí
Tuesday	Úterý
Wednesday	Středa
Thursday	Čtvrtek
Friday	Pátek
Saturday	Sobota
Sunday	Neděle
Open	Otevřeno
Closed	Zavřeno
No entry	Vstup zakázán
Smoking prohibited	Kouření zakázáno

Woman / Women	Žena / Ženy
Man / Men	Muž / Muži
Name	Jméno
Adress	Adresa
Date of birth	Datum narození
Documents	Dokumenty
Ticket *(bus/train e.t.c.)*	Jízdenka

BASIC NUMBERS	
1	Jedna
2	Dvě
3	Tři
4	Čtyři
5	Pět
6	Šest
7	Sedm
8	Osm
9	Devět
10	Deset
100	Sto
1 000	Tisíc

GETTING ACQUAINTED	
What´s your name?	Jak se jmenujete?
My name is …	Jmenuji se …
Where are you from?	Odkud jste?
I´m from …	Jsem z …
Are you from Prague?	Jste z Prahy?

ORIENTATION	
Left	Vlevo
Right	Napravo
Straight on	Rovně
Where is …?	Kde je …?
Station	Nádraží
Airport	Letiště
Underground/Subway	Metro
Tourist information	Turistické informace
Square	Náměstí

Pharmacy	Lékárna
Hospital	Nemocnice
Emergency service	Pohotovost
Police Station	Policejní stanice
Street ...	Ulice ...
Grocery store	Potraviny
Toilets	Toalety
Post Office	Pošta
Bank	Banka
Exchange Office	Směnárna
Bus stop	Stanice
How far is it?	Jak je to daleko?
IN SHOPS AND RESTAURANTS	
How much is it?	Kolik to stojí?
Write the price for me please.	Napište mi cenu, prosím.
Price	Cena
I´d like to pay please.	Zaplatím
I like that.	To se mi líbí
I don´t like that.	To se mi nelíbí
Small	Malý
Big	Velký
Expensive	Drahý

Cheap	Levný
Discount	Sleva
Can I try it?	Mohu to zkusit?
TOAST	
Cheers!	Na zdraví!

Dva (Two)

Tři (Three)

107

Hotel Prague

IL GIARDINO RESTAURANT
Mozartova 261/1
Praha 5, 150 00
Tel.: +420 257 154 262
hotel.prague@moevenpick.com

This modern Italian restaurant, with a large outdoor terrace overlooking the City of Prague, is located on the top of the Mrazovka Hill, at the executive building of the Mövenpick Hotel. The restaurant is accessible from the main hotel building via unique cable car, operating year round. Sunday family brunches every Sunday from 11:30 am till 3 pm.

AMERICKÝ BAR
p. 132
D4
Náměstí Republiky 5, 110 00 Praha 1
Tel.: +420 222 002 770
sales@francouzskarestaurace.cz
www.francouzskarestaurace.cz

- *The oldest bar in Prague coming from 1912*
- *Sophisticated and intimate atmosphere*
- *Wide selection of cocktails and drinks*

PLZEŇSKÁ RESTAURACE
(PLZENSKA RESTAURANT)
p. 132
D4
Náměstí Republiky 5, 110 00 Praha 1
Tel.: +420 222 002 770
sales@plzenskarestaurace.cz
www.plzenskarestaurace.cz

- *Located in the basement of the Municipal House*
- *Traditional Czech cuisine*
- *Excellent Pilsner beer*
- *Courteous and friendly service*
- *Daily live folklore music*

FRANCOUZSKÁ RESTAURACE
(FRANCOUZSKA RESTAURANT)
p. 132
D4
Náměstí Republiky 5, 110 00 Praha 1
Tel.: +420 222 002 770
sales@francouzskarestaurace.cz
www.francouzskarestaurace.cz

- *The most beautiful Art Nouveau restaurant in the world*
  Located in the right wing of the Municipal House
- *Daily live music*
- *International and Czech cuisine*
- *Premium caterer of the President of the Czech Republic*

RESTAURANT ASTRA
IN AQUAPALACE HOTEL **** PRAGUE
Pražská 137, 251 01 Čestlice
Prague – East
Tel.: +420 225 108 888
Fax: +420 225 108 999
info@aquapalacehotel.cz

www.aquapalacehotel.cz

Enjoy the best of our wide selection of Czech and international specialties in the hotel restaurant „Astra". Terrace dining is another perfect choice for a special dining experience, whether for a refreshing breakfast or a romantic dinner. For our little guests, we have created a number of special children´s meals.

p. 133
D3

RESTAURANT U MODRÉ RŮŽE
(AT THE BLUE ROSE RESTAURANT)
Prague 1, Rytířská 16
Tel.: + 420 224 225 873
Tel./fax: + 420 224 222 623
restaurant@umodreruze.cz
www.umodreruze.cz

- Czech and international extra special gastronomy
- Moravian, French, Spanish, Italian and Chilean wine
- intimate, exclusive 15th century atmosphere
- Evening preludes produced by our pianists
- VISA, AMEX, DC, EC/MC, JCB

p. 137
D4

half & half

HALF & HALF
Václavské náměstí 51, Praha 1
Tel.: +420 222 240 696
Mobil: +420 724 827 508
jannisfood@email.cz
www. halfandhalf.cz

- Greek Specialities (Gyros, Moussaka, Gemista) • Genuine Italian pizza prepared according to authentic recipes • 30 flavours of Italian ice cream (homemade) • Production of cakes, desserts and confectionery • Fresh, homemade noodles with your favourite sauces • Authentic Belgian truffles • Genuine Greek frappe • A wide selection of salads • Stuffed baguettes, paninis, ciabattas, bagels • Outstanding coffee (Caffe Perrero) • WI-FI ZONE

mon. – sun.: 7.00 am – 12.00 midnight

All of our products are made by us from authentic ingredients.

p. 137
D4

RESTAURACE JÁMA
V Jámě 7, Praha 1
Tel.: +420 224 222 383
open: 11.00 – 1.00
www.jamapub.cz

The best pub in Prague – The Prague Post, 2008

One of the city´s – very best hamburgers – The Prague Post, Jan 13 2005

Prague´s Best Burger – www.prague.tv, 2004

Some of the best – burgers in town — avantguide Prague, 2004

CZECH CUISINE

Lokal

p. 144
C3

LOKAL
Praha 1, Dlouhá 33
Tel.: +420 222 316 265
lokal@ambi.cz
www.ambi.cz

mon. – fri.	11:00 am	– 01:00 pm
sat.	12:00 noon	– 01:00 pm
sun.	12:00 noon	– 10:00 pm

The restaurant presents honest home-style Czech meals. The chefs prepare the dishes from fresh ingredients produced by reputable regional suppliers. You enjoy Czech cuisine with draught Pilsner Urquell beer – from the tank straight into a pint glass.

TEX MEX CUISINE

AMBIENTE
THE LIVING RESTAURANT

p. 138
E4

**AMBIENTE
– THE LIVING RESTAURANTS**
Praha 2, Mánesova 59
Tel.: +420 222 727 851
manesova@ambi.cz
www.ambi.cz

mon. – fri.	11.00 am	– 12.00 pm
sat. – sun.	12.00 noon	– 12.00 pm

This restaurant in the heart of Royal Vinohrady offers informal dining and American Tex-Mex cuisine. Renowned for its baked ribs, grilled wings, and steaks from the best beef prepared precisely the way you like it. Outstanding staff to serve you. A restaurant that is alive!

BRAZILIAN CUISINE

AMBIENTE
RESTAURANTE BRASILERO

p. 133
D3

**AMBIENTE
– RESTAURANTE BRASILEIRO**
Praha1, U Radnice 8
Tel.: +420 224 234 474
brasileiro@ambi.cz

p. 134
D4

Na Příkopě 22, Praha 1
Tel.: +420 221 451 200
slovanskydum@ambi.cz,
www.ambi.cz

mon.–sun.	11.00 am	– 12.00 pm
mon.–sun.	12.00 noon	– 12.00 pm

Two restaurants with authentic Brazilian cuisine – genuine churrasco-rodizio. In addition to grilled meat from select South American bulls, you can treat yourself to the specialities from the salad bar such as sushi, typical Brazilian vegetable dishes and seafood and enjoy "all you can eat" for a single price of CZK 625.

ITALIAN CUISINE

AMBIENTE
RISTORANTE PASTA FRESCA

p. 133
D3

**AMBIENTE
– RISTORANTE PASTA FRESCA**
Celetná 11, Praha 1
Tel.: +420 224 230 244
celetna@ambi.cz,
www.ambi.cz

restaurant	mon. – sun.	11.00 am–12.00 pm
café	mon. – sun.	10.00 am–12.00 pm

This Italian restaurant located in a beautiful Gothic cellar prepares dishes from fresh homemade pastas according to recipes from the best regions of Italy. It has a large selection of more than 200 kinds of wines. Three experienced sommeliers shall gladly help you select the right wine.

p. 133 D3

p. 133 C3

ITALIAN CUISINE

Tonino Lamborghini
PASTACAFFÉ

PASTACAFFÉ LAMBORGHINI
Vodičkova 8, Praha 1
Tel.: +420 222 231 869
vodickova@ambi.cz

Vězeňská 1, Prague 1
Tel.: +420 224 813 257
vezenska@ambi.cz
www.ambi.cz

| mon. – sat. | 08.00 am –10.00 pm |
| sun. | 10.00 am –10.00 pm |

Two modern-design theme cafés in the centre of Prague offer a large selection of coffees, a rich breakfast menu and light Italian dishes. The ideal place to enjoy your morning coffee.

---

p. 134 C4

ITALIAN CUISINE

AMBIENTE
RISTORANTE PIZZA NUOVA

AMBIENTE – PIZZA NUOVA
Revoluční 1, Praha 1
Tel.: +420 221 803 308
pizzanuova@ambi.cz
www.ambi.cz

| mon. – sun. | 11.30 am –11.30 pm |

This restaurant prepares selected pasta specialities in addition to luscious Neapolitan pizzas. It also offers grilled meats and fresh fish. You can choose from an "a la carte" menu or "all you can eat" pizza & pasta for a single price of CZK 328. The children's corner is open daily, with supervision on the weekends.

---

p. 136 D2

CZECH-FRENCH CUISINE

CAFÉ 1893 **SAVOY**

CAFÉ SAVOY
Vítězná 5, Praha 5
Tel.: +420 257 311 562
savoy@ambi.cz
www.ambi.cz

| mon. – fri. | 8.00 am – 10.30 pm |
| sat. – sun. | 9.00 am – 10.30 pm |

This café restaurant with a monument-protected Neo-Renaissance ceiling has a tradition dating back to 1893. When you enter, you shall be enveloped by the atmosphere of Prague's café tradition at the turn of the 20th century. You can enjoy the best of traditional Czech cuisine served with French refinement. Rich breakfasts, homemade confectionery and desserts made by a master chef are very popular.

---

p. 134 C4

CZECH HAUTE CUISINE

LA DEGUSTATION
BOHÈME BOURGEOISE

LA DEGUSTATION BOHÊME BOURGEOISE
Haštalská 18, Praha 1
Tel.: + 420 222 311 234
boheme@ambi.cz,
www.ladegustation.cz

| mon. – sat. | 06.00 pm | – | 12.00 pm |
| tue., wed., thu. | 12.00 noon | – | 02.30 pm |

This unique tasting restaurant prepares 2 tasting menus consisting in seven courses supplemented by a seventh amuse-bouche. The head chef, Oldřich Sahajdák, prepares traditional dishes from Czech culinary art at the end of the 19th century inspired by the masterfully created recipes of culinary expert Marie B. Svobodová.

Mon. – Sun.: 12.00 am – 12.00 pm

U KRKAVCŮ
Dlouhá 24
110 00 Prague 1
Tel.: +420 224 817264
Fax: +420 222 329 121
info@u-krkavcu.cz
www.u-krkavcu.cz

p. 133
C3

Wine restaurant in the historical centre of Prague under vaulted roman ceilings offers rich choice of czech and international entertainment.

SUSHI BAR
Zborovská 49
150 00 Praha 5
Malá Strana
Tel.: 603 244 882
sushi@sushi.cz
www.sushi.cz

CLASSIFIED AS THE BEST JAPANESE RESTAURANT IN THE CZECH REPUBLIC.

TERASA U ZLATÉ STUDNĚ
U Zlaté studně 166/4
118 00 Praha 1 – Malá Strana
Tel.: +420 257 533 322
restaurant@zlatastudna.cz
www.terasauzlatestudne.cz

p. 132
C2

Come discover the magic of the most beautiful hidden treasure in Lesser Town – the "TERASA U Zlaté studně" restaurant. Enjoy selected delicacies seasoned by a fantastic view of Prague! The head chef, Pavel Sapík, and his team create culinary works of art. The gardens of Prague Castle are directly accessible from the restaurant. This served as the personal entrance for Emperor Rudolf II.

THE NEW TOWN BREWERY RESTAURANT

NOVOMĚSTSKÝ PIVOVAR
Vodičkova 20, 110 00 Praha 1
Tel., fax: +420 222 232 448
+420 222 231 662
+420 602 459 216
sales@npivovar.cz,
www.npivovar.cz

p. 137
D3

An unique gastronomical rarity in Prague!

400 seats
The opportunity to watch the actual brewing of our own 11° lager
Typical Czech cooking
Tour of the brewery
The beer parties with live music   ***OPEN DAILY***

p. 137
D4

RESTAURACE VÝTOPNA
Václavské náměstí 56
110 00 Praha 1
Tel.: +420 725 190 646
praha.vaclavak@vytopna.cz

Not only is the Výtopna Restaurant a pleasant place to stop for a while for railway lovers: it is attractive for anybody who loves good food. This gastronomic original will change even a one-beer-stop into a truly unforgettable experience. The restaurant is equipped with little model trains that move along a 400-metre-long track. The trains will deliver your drinks right to your table and without delay! The Výtopna Restaurant is provided with modern air-conditioning. Wi-fi connections to the internet are free of charge.

www.vytopna.cz

Restaurant
Gourmet

**RESTAURANT GOURMET
CLARION CONGRESS
HOTEL PRAGUE******
Freyova 33, CZ – 190 00
Prague 9 – Vysočany
Tel.: + 420 211 131 222
fb.cchp@clarion-hotels.cz
www.clarion-hotels.cz
www.clarioncongresshotelprague.com

Fine Dining Restaurant Gourmet offers an attractive and cosy atmosphere for an excellent evening out. Tasty and delicious dishes prepared by master chefs represent the global modern gastronomy. The culinary experience is supported by the offer of quality wines of world production from renowned wineries.

p. 136
D2

TLUSTÁ MYŠ

TLUSTÁ MYŠ (FAT MOUSE PUB)
Restaurant, bar & little gallery
Všehrdova 19, Prague 1, Malá Strana
Tel.: +420 257 320 409, +420 605 282 506
www.fatmousepub.com

This small pub and little gallery has a pleasant atmosphere and interior where you can taste excellent Pilsner beer or Moravian wine at very reasonable prices. At the same time you can fill your empty stomachs with our specialities, delicious steaks or pickled camembert.
Open daily: Mo.–Fri.:11.30–00.00
Sa.: 12.00–00.00
Su.: 12.00–22.00

p. 137
D3

KÁVA · KÁVA · KÁVA
· Praha 1, courtyard Platýz,
Národní 37; tel: 224 228 862
E-mail: kava@mbox.vol.cz
www.kava-coffee.cz

· Praha 5, Nový Smíchov – Anděl,
Lidická 42; tel.: 257 314 277
E-mail: kava@magicware.cz

· Coffee to-go
· Wi-Fi hotspot
· High speed Internet

THE BEST COFFEE IN PRAGUE!
Light meals all day + international cuisine + beer on tap

AQUAPALACE RESORT PRAGUE
Pražská 137, 251 01 Čestlice
Prague – East
Tel.: +420 225 108 888
Fax: +420 225 108 999
info@aquapalacehotel.cz

www.aquapalacehotel.cz

Located in AQUAPALACE PRAHA, Central Europe's largest Aquapark, the 4-star Aquapalace Hotel provides the perfect ground for business and physical well being in one of the most beautiful European capitals.

MÖVENPICK HOTEL PRAGUE
Mozartova 261/1
Praha 5, 150 00
Tel.: +420 257 153 111
Fax: +420 257 153 131
hotel.prague@moevenpick.com

www.moevenpick-prague.com

The Mövenpick Hotel Prague is a prime destination for corporate and leisure travelers thanks to its location in the city centre, first rate service based on Swiss quality and professional event management. Hotel consists of two separate buildings connected by a unique cable car and offers 442 rooms with superb views over the Prague.

HOTEL ČERTOVKA
U Lužického semináře 2
110 00 Praha 1
Tel.: +420 257 011 500
Fax: +420 257 534 392
reservations@certovka.cz
URL: www.certovka.cz

p. 132 D2

- *this 4* hotel is located in the Lesser Town, directly besid the Charles Bridge*
- *16 double and 5 single comfortably equipped rooms*
- *breakfast in the form of a cold and hot buffet*
- *a guarded underground car park not far from the hotel*

petra mechurova®
HAIR DESIGN

SALON PETRA MĚCHUROVÁ
Králodvorská 12
110 10 Prague 1, Česká republika
Tel.: +420 224 222 442
salon@petra.mechurova.cz
www.petra.mechurova.cz

p. 133 D4

- *attractively situated salon in the centre of Prague near the Royal Way*
- *we use L'ORÉAL PROFESSIONNEL and KÉRASTASE cosmetics*
- *professional care of your appearance*

p. 133
D4

PALLADIUM
náměstí Republiky
Prague 1, (metro line B)
Tel.: +420 225 770 250
infokiosek@palladiumpraha.cz
www.palladiumpraha.cz

- 180 shops
- 20 restaurants, bars & cafés
- Open 7 days a week
- Right downtown Prague
- 900 underground parking spaces

---

p. 133
C4

p. 137
D4

p. 134
C4

THAI FIT

- *THAI, OIL, HERB, REFLEXIVE,
  AND PEELING MASSAGES*
- *SAUNA*
- *TANNING SALON*
- *THAI RESTAURANT*

OPEN DAILY 9.00 AM – 9.00 PM

THAI FIT
Na Poříčí 21, 110 00 Praha 1
(near the shopping centre (Bílé labutě))
Tel.: 224 811 876, 224 811 872
Mobil: 603 490 247
Vodičkova 41, 110 00 Praha 1
(Světozor gallery passage)
Tel.: 224 152 016, 224 947 539
Mobil: 739 516 404
Petrská 23, 110 00 Praha 1
Tel.: 224 815 253, 224 815 281,
Mobil: 733 501 277

www.thaifit.cz

---

p. 137
E4

OPEN
MO. – FR.: 9.00–19.00
SA.:   10.00–15.00

BAZAR CD, LP, DVD
Krakovská 4, PRAHA 1
Krakovská 2, PRAHA 1
Tel.: 602 313 730
777 043 778

— *THE BEST AND THE BIGGEST IN CZECHOSLOVAKIA*
— *PERMANENT OFFER OF 50 000 CDs OF ALL TYPES*
— *ONLY ORIGINAL CDs, VINYLs, DVDs*
— *150 METRES FROM WENCESLAS SQUARE*
— *RARITIES, BOOTLEGS AND SO ON.*
— *DISCOUNTS AVAILABLE*
— *DAILY CASH PURCHASES*
— *ON-LINE ORDERS*

---

p. 136
D2

OPEN
MO. – FR.: 10.00 – 20.00
SA.:   10.00 – 19.00
SU.:   13.00 – 19.00

BAZAR CD, LP, DVD
Vítězná 18
PRAHA 1 – ÚJEZD
Tel.: 608 843 535

— *PERMANENT OFFER OF 10 000 CDs*
— *JAZZ, ROCK, POP, CZECHOSLOVAKIAN SCENE....*
— *ONLY ORIGINAL CDs, VINYLs, DVDs*
— *RARITIES, BOOTLEGS AND SO ON.*
— *DAILY CASH PURCHASES*
— *ON-LINE ORDERS*
— *CONSULTATION WITH SPECIALIST STAFF*

SERVICES

CAFE EBEL
Kaprová 11, Praha 1
Tel.: +420 604 265 125
mo–fr: 8–19, sa–su: 10–19
Wi-Fi

p. 133
D3

p. 133
D4

CAFE EBEL
Řetězová 9, Praha 1
Tel.: +420 603 823 665
mo–su: 8–20
Wi-Fi

CAFE EBEL
Templová 7, Praha 1
Tel.: +420 603 544 492
Wi-Fi

We prepare freshly roasted coffee made from raw coffee beans imported from all the world's coffee plantations every week.
We work exclusively with the highest quality beans because the resulting Ebel coffee is extraordinarily aromatic and tasty.

www.ebelcoffee.cz

VIVA PRAHA
Celetná 10
110 00 Praha 1
Tel.: 0042 224 242 952
info@vivapraha.cz
www.viva4you.com

p. 133
D4

Viva Praha offers all chocolate lovers the best from Belgian chocolate makers. In the centre of Prague not far from Old Town Square you can visit a kingdom of traditional Belgian truffles and marzipan, nougat, and last but not least, sugar bonbons, which you can see being made right in the shop.

Open daily: 10.30 am – 10.30 pm

PRAGUE CASTLE
PRAG ART COLLECTION S. R. O.
Střední trakt Nového paláce
(Middle wing of the New Palace)
Tel./fax: +420 224 372 259

p. 132
D2

- Breathtaking shop in the historical part of the castle
- Tourist assortment
- All about Prague and about the castle

PRAGUE CASTLE
PRAG ART COLLECTION S. R. O.
Starý Královský palác
(Old Royal Palace)
Zelená Světnice
(Green Chamber)
Tel./fax: +420 224 372 259

p. 132
D2

- Information leaflets and brochures about the history of the city and the castle
- Theme gifts for travellers, postcards, calendars, guidebooks, etc.
- Refreshments

AQUAPALACE RESORT PRAGUE
Pražská 137, 251 01 Čestlice
Prague – East
Tel.: +420 225 108 888
Fax: +420 225 108 999
info@aquapalacehotel.cz

Sports, relaxation and joy from a stay by the water. All of this is offered to you by Aquapalace Praha – the largest aquapark in Central Europe, which is located in the immediate vicinity of the Aquapalace Hotel and is connected to it via a connecting tunnel.

www.aquapalace.cz
www. aquapalacehotel.cz

---

p. 132
D2

SEGWAY EXPERIENCE
Mostecká 4
Praha 1 – Malá strana
Tel.: +420 731 238 264
Fax: +420 271 742 419
info@segwayfun.eu

Come and explore Prague from the SEGWAY perspective on the Prague segway tour! Slide 20 cm above the ground wherever you wish. You can have a unique opportunity to see the most appealing sites in Prague on segway in only 3 hours. Forget buses, cars, bicycles! Step on the SEGWAY and have fun with us!

www.segwayfun.eu

PŮJČOVNA LODIČEK
(BOAT RENTAL)
Praha Smíchov
Praha Staré město
Tel.: +420 739 000 022
info@pujcovna-lodicek.cz
www.pujcovnalodicek.cz

Come and hire motorboats, punts, a pleasure catamaran with a grill, or a Chinese junk.

BOTANICKÁ ZAHRADA PRAHA
(PRAGUE BOTANIC GARDENS)
Nádvorní 134
Prague 7 – Troja
Tel.: +420/234 148 111
info@botanicka.cz
www.botanicka.cz

*Connections:
bus 112 from Nádraží Holešovice underground station to ZOO or Botanická zahrada Troja stations, from there along the marked routes.*

NÁRODNÍ GALERIE V PRAZE
(NATIONAL GALLERY IN PRAGUE)
www.ngprague.cz

p. 133
D3

Open daily except Mondays from 10.00 till 18.00.

St. George´s Convent is open to the public daily from 10.00 till 18.00.

ŠTERNBERSKÝ PALÁC
(STERNBERG PALACE)
Hradčanské nám. 15
118 01 Praha 1

p. 132
C1

ARTE EUROPEO DESDE LA EDAD ANTIGUA
HASTA FINALES DEL BARROCO

tram nr. 22 – *Pražský hrad* station
metro A – *Malostranská* station
tram nr. 12, 18, 20, 22 – *Malostranská* station

KLÁŠTER SV. ANEŽKY ČESKÉ
(CONVENT OF ST. AGNES OF BOHEMIA)
U Milosrdných 17
110 00 Praha 1 – Staré Město

p. 133
C3

MEDIEVAL ART IN BOHEMIA AND CENTRAL EUROPE

metro A – *Staroměstská* station
metro B – *Náměstí Republiky* station
tram nr. 5, 8, 14, 26 – *Dlouhá* station
tram nr. 17 – *Právnická fakulta* station

VALDŠTEJNSKÁ JÍZDÁRNA
(WALDSTEIN RIDING
SCHOOL GALLERY)
Valdštejnská 3
118 01 Praha 1

p. 133
C2

ČESKÝ SENÁT
USTAVEN V ROCE 1996

EXTRAORDINARY PROJECTS ORGANIZED AND HELD
IN COOPERATION WITH THE SENATE
OF THE PARLIAMENT OF THE CZECH REPUBLIC.

metro A – *Malostranská* station
tram nr. 12, 18, 20, 22 – *Malostranská* station

CULTURE

p. 133
D4

DŮM U ČERNÉ MATKY BOŽÍ
(HOUSE AT THE BLACK MADONA)
Ovocný trh 19
110 00 Prague 1 – Staré Město

CZECH CUBISM 1910–1919

tram nr. 5, 8, 14, 26 – Náměstí Republiky station
metro A – Můstek station
metro B – Náměstí Republiky station

p. 132
C2

KLÁŠTER SV. JIŘÍ
(ST. GEORGE´S CONVENT
MONASTERY)
Jiřské nám. 33
119 00 Prague 1 – Castle

ART OF THE 19TH CENTURY IN BOHEMIA

tram nr. 22 – Pražský hrad station
metro A and tram nr. 12, 18, 20, 22 – Malostranská station

p. 134
B4

VELETRŽNÍ PALÁC
(VELETRŽNÍ PALACE)
Dukelských hrdinů 47
170 00 Prague 7 – Holešovice

ART OF THE 20TH AND 21ST CENTURIES

tram nr. 1, 5, 8, 12, 14, 17, 25, 26 – Strossmayerovo nám. station
metro C – Vltavská station

p. 132
C1

SCHWARZENBERSKÝ PALÁC
(SCHWARZENBERG PALACE)
Hradčanské nám. 2
118 00 Praha 1

BAROQUE IN BOHEMIA

tram nr. 22 – Pražský hrad station

 Národní divadlo

LATERNA MAGIKA
p. 137
D3

Tickets: NEW STAGE cash desk
Národní 4, Prague 1
Tel.: 224 931 482
novascena@narodni-divadlo.cz
www.laterna.cz

*THE LEGENDARY MULTIMEDIA THEATRE IN THE VERY
HEART OF PRAGUE
5 GREAT MULTIMEDIA PERFORMANCES
NO LANGUAGE BARRIER
PERFORMANCES FOR KIDS AND MUCH MORE*

CHOCO-STORY
THE CHOCOLATE MUSEUM
p. 133
D4

Celetná 10
110 00 Praha 1
Tel.: 0042 224 242 953
info@choco-story-praha.cz
www.choco-story-praha.cz

Open daily: 10.30 am – 7.00 pm

The Choco-Story Museum offers its visitors a look at the 3,000 year history of the production of chocolate, starting with ancient civilizations and ending with modern methods of production. Come with the chocolate fairy and engulf yourself in a jungle where the cacao tree grows and allow yourself to be carried away by the sweet taste and aroma of chocolate.

 FUTURISTAUNIVERSUM

FUTURISTA UNIVERSUM
ARCHITECTURE AND DESIGN
p. 133
D3

Betlémské nám. 5a
110 00 Praha 1
Tel.: 00420 725 128 660
www.futurista.cz
futurista@futurista.cz

We invite you to the newly opened centre for contemporary architecture, design and art, which is located in the heart of historic Prague very near the Bethlehem Chapel.

 KUBISTA

GALERIE KUBISTA
p. 133
D4

Dům U Černé Matky Boží
Ovocný trh 19
110 00 Praha 1
Tel./fax: +420 224 236 378
kubista@kubista.cz
www.kubista.cz

• unique dealer in the centre of Prague
• applied art replicas and originals from the first half of the 20th century.
• Cubist boxes, coffee sets, vases and furniture, jewellery
• collection of posters and postcards with Cubist architecture

CULTURE

---

p. 133
C3

Annelies Štrba – Rudolfinum

Opening hours:
Tuesday–Wednesday, Friday–Sunday: 10:00 – 18:00
Thursday: 10:00 – 20:00

galerie@rudolfinum.org
www.galerierudolfinum.org

GALERIE RUDOLFINUM
Alšovo nábřeží 12
Cz – 110 00 Prague 1
Tel.: +420 227 059 205
Fax: +420 222 319 293

Galerie Rudolfinum brings top contemporary art from around the world to Prague. Exhibitions of Damien Hirst, Andy Warhol, Gregory Drewson, Georg Baselitz or Chinese Painting are just a few of examples of the recent offer to visitors from this state, non-profit "kunsthalle". Galerie Rudolfinum exhibitions also make occasional excursions into periods of more distant history. Don't miss this unique opportunity to meet art in Prague.

Galerie Rudolfinum is administered by the Museum of Decorative Arts in Prague.

---

p. 133
D3

IMAGE THEATRE
Pařížská 4, Prague 1
Tel.: +420 222 314 448
+420 222 329 191
Fax: +420 224 811 167
image@imagetheatre.cz
www.imagetheatre.cz.

BLACK LIGHT THEATRE
PANTOMIME
MODERN DANCE

Daily performances at 8 p.m.

---

p. 132
D2

Muzeum pověstí a strašidel

**PRAGUE GHOSTS
& LEGENDS MUSEUM**
Mostecká 18, Praha 1
www.ghostmuseumprague.cz

Open daily
1 0:00 – 22:00

- Experience the mystery of Old Prague
- Discover original Prague ghost stories
- Wander the underground street of ghosts
- Enjoy an interactive exposition
- Meet the ghosts face to face

O2 ŽLUTÉ LÁZNĚ
Podolské nábřeží 1
147 00 Praha 4 – Podolí
Reservation: +420 244 463 777
info@taiko.cz, www.o2zlutelazne.cz

Multifunctional complex O2 žluté lázně on the bank of the Vltava River is an ideal place for leisure.
Sports: football in a cage, pétanque football-tennis, table tennis, beach volleyball, motor boats, pedal boats, dragon boats, boats, rental in-line skates, external giant chess.
Food specialties: wide range of cocktails, grilled specialities, czech and international cuisine.

MELANTRICHOVA

ŽELEZNÁ

STAROMĚSTSKÉ NÁM.

CELETNÁ

DLOUHÁ

1/ Charles Bridge
2/ Lesser Town Bridge Tower
3/ St. Nicholas Church
4/ Malostranské square
5/ Church of St. Thomas
6/ Smiřický Palace
7/ Lichtenštejnský Palace

SNĚMOVNÍ

MOSTECKÁ

page 76

ČERTOVKA

NA KAMPĚ

RECOMMENDED WEB PAGES

www.czech.cz *(The Official Website of the Czech Republic)*

www.prague-info.cz *(Prague Information Service)*

www.hrad.cz/en *(Prague Castle)*

www.pribeh-hradu.cz *(Exhibitions, tours and cultural events at Prague Castle)*

www.praha-mesto.cz *(Prague City Hall information server)*

www.prague-portal.com *(All about Prague)*

www.nm.cz/english *(The National Museum)*

www.muzeumprahy.cz *(Museum of the Capital City of Prague)*

www.jewishmuseum.cz *(The Jewish Museum in Prague)*

www.ngprague.cz *(The National Gallery in Prague)*

www.narodni-divadlo.cz *(The National Theatre)*

www.czechphilharmonic.cz/en *(The Czech Philharmonic Orchestra)*

www.laterna.cz *(Laterna Magika Theatre)*

www.zoopraha.cz *(Prague Zoo)*

www.botanicka.cz *(Prague Botanical Garden)*

www.loreta.cz *(Loreta Pilgrim Place)*

www.strahovskyklaster.cz *(Royal Canonry of Premonstratensians at Strahov)*

www.cuni.cz *(Charles University)*

www.obecnidum.cz *(The Municipal House)*

www.evd.cz *(Boat trips)*

www.premiant.cz *(City tours)*

www.citytaxi.cz *(Prague Taxi Service)*

www.czechairlines.com *(Czech Airlines)*

www.idos.cz *(National Timetable Information System)*

ww.jizdnirady.atlas.cz *(National Timetable Information System)*

www.rentcentral.cz *(Car rental)*

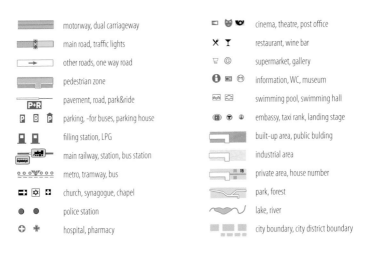

motorway, dual carriageway

main road, traffic lights

other roads, one way road

pedestrian zone

pavement, road, park&ride

parking, -for buses, parking house

filling station, LPG

main railway, station, bus station

metro, tramway, bus

church, synagogue, chapel

police station

hospital, pharmacy

cinema, theatre, post office

restaurant, wine bar

supermarket, gallery

information, WC, museum

swimming pool, swimming hall

embassy, taxi rank, landing stage

built-up area, public bulding

industrial area

private area, house number

park, forest

lake, river

city boundary, city district boundary

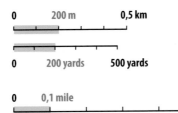

0   200 m   0,5 km

0   200 yards   500 yards

0   0,1 mile   0,5 mile

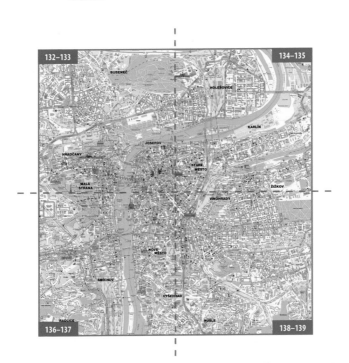

132–133   134–135

BUBENEČ

HOLEŠOVICE

KARLÍN

JOSEFOV

HRADČANY

STARÉ MĚSTO

MALÁ STRANA

ŽIŽKOV

VINOHRADY

NOVÉ MĚSTO

SMÍCHOV

VYŠEHRAD

RADLICE

NUSLE

136–137   138–139

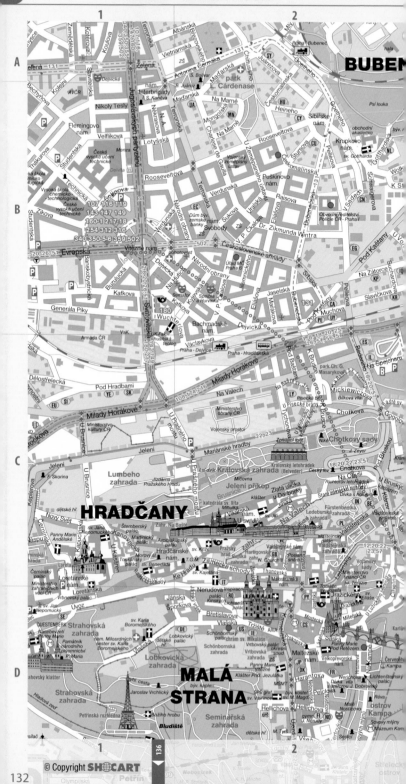

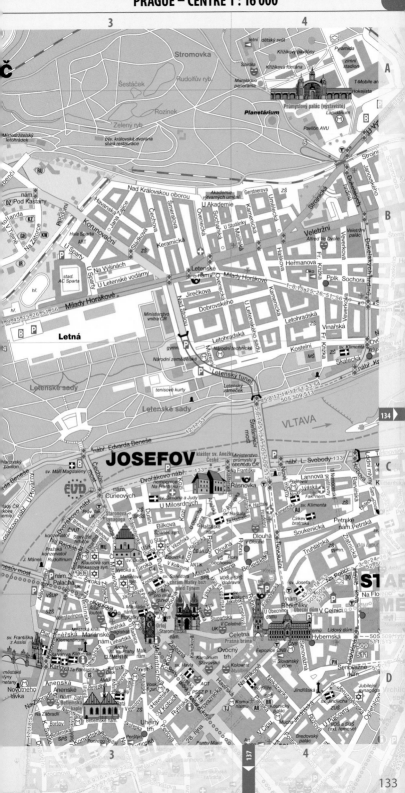

Č

Stromovka

Šestáček

Rudolfův ryb.

Rozinek

Zelený ryb.

letní dětský svět
Křižíkovy pavilóny
Pyramida
Šírala
Křižíkova fontána
zimní
stadion
Maroldovo
panoráma
T-Mobile ar
Hokejista
Planetárium
Průmyslový palác (výstaviště)
Lapidárium
Pavilón AVU

Místodržitelský
letohrádek

Nad Královskou oborou
Akademie
výtvarných umění
Gerstnerova ZŠ
U Akademie
U Studánky
Veletržní
Veletržní
palác
Alfred Ve Dvoře

nám.
Pod Kaštany

Havanská
Korunovační
Šmeralova
Ovenecká
Sochařská
Malířská
Haškova
Heřmanova
Oko
Pplk. Sochora
Veverkova
Dukelských hrdinů

Hala Sparta
ART
Keramická
ZŠ
U Sparty

stad.
AC Sparta
hř.
U Vyšíhách
Na Výšinách
U Letenské vodárny
Letenské
nám.
Jirečkova
Milady Horákové
Dobrovského
U Letenského sadu
Letohradská
Vinařská
Fr. Křížka

Milady Horákové
Nad Štolou
Letohradská
Kostelní
sv. Klimenta
Skalecká
nábř. Kr

Letná
Ministerstvo
vnitra ČR
gymn.
Národní technické
Národní zeměměřické
MŠ
Letenský tunel
Letenský
zámeček

Lětenské sady
tenisové kurty

Letenské sady
Štefánikův
most
VLTAVA

nábř. Edvarda Beneše
sv. Máří Magdalény
JOSEFOV
klášter sv. Anežky
České
nábř. L. Svobody – 133
Lannova

134 ▶

sv. Maří Magdalény
Dvořákovo nábř. – 133
Na Františku
Ministerstvo
průmyslu a obchodu ČR
Na Františku
Rásnovka
Pošťovní
Nemocnice
Na Františku
Lannova
Lásská
Fak. nem.
Lidní mlýny
AU

nám.
Curieových
sv. Simona a Judy
U Milosrdných
Kozí
Haštalské
nám.
Za Haštalem
Klimentská
sv. Klimenta
Petrské
nám. Petrská
ZŠ
Bílá Labuť

Dušní
Bilkova
Haštalská
Dlouhá
Rybná
Církev
bratrská
Soukenická
Truhlářská
ZŠ
gymn.
Zlatnická
S

Staronová
synagoga
Vězeňská
Bíln. U Salvátora
Kozí
Dlouhá
VS Roxy
obchodní
Revoluční
Na Poříčí
STAF
ME

Široká
Kaprova
Pinkasova syn.
Maiselova
Dušní
Vysoká
Masná
Masná
Benediktská
VOS a SPŠS
dopravní
sv. Josefa
Petrské
nám.
Republiky
Obecní dům
U Celnici
Lidový dům

nám.
Palacha
Pařížská
Maiselova
Široká
chrám Matky boží
před Týnem
Jakubská
U Obecního
domu

Klausová syn.
UK
Jáchymova
Staroměstské
nám.
Celetná
Celetná
Exposice ČNB

Mánesův most
ŠUP
UK
Mikulaše
Orloj
Staroměstská
radnice
Prašná brána
Hybernská

nám.
Jana Palacha
Městská knih.
Klementinum
Platnéřská
Linhartská
Karlova
Brány
Melantrichova
Železná
Ovocný
trh
Karolinum
Stavovské
Kolowrat
Slovanský
dům
Senovážné
nám.
PH

sv. Františka
z Assisi
509
511

Anenská
nám. Zlaté
Karlova
Ta Fantastická
Karlova
IS
Havelská
Havelská
Na Příkopě
Nekázanka
Jindřišská
Jubilejní
synagoga

Novotného
lávka
městské
mlýny
SZŠ

Anenská
nám. Zlaté
Betlémská
kaple
Betlémské nám.
ZŠ
Vejvodova
Michalská
AG
V Kotcích
Rytířská
sv. Jiljí
SPŠ
Komorní
Jindřišská
Mucha palác
U Půlcovny
VOS a SUŠ
(text. řemesla)

Náprstkova
Na Zábradlí
Konviktská
SPŠ
Uhelný
trh
28. října
Panty Marie
BR
J.
AR
Opletalova

Komenského
Perštýn
Skořepka
Art
Bredovský
dvůr

▲ 137

133

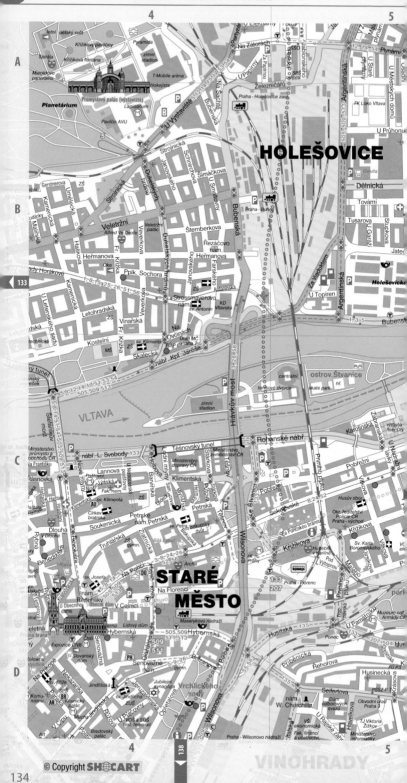

HOLEŠOVICE

STARÉ MĚSTO

VLTAVA

ostrov Štvanice

VINOHRADY

KARLÍN

ŽIŽKOV

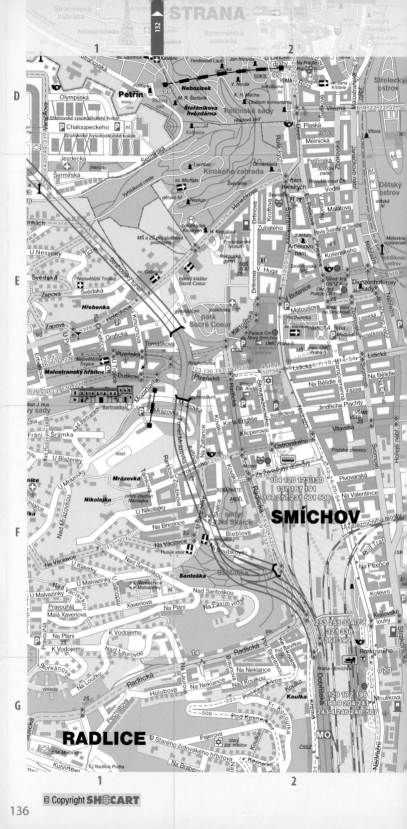

6
7

D

Olšanské hřbitovy

E

Olšanská
Táborská
Olšanské nám.
sv. Rocha

SOŠ
obchodní
akademie
Kubelíkova
Chvalova

Starý Židovský
olšanský hřbitov
Televizní věž
Žižkov
Žižkovo nám.
SUPŠ

Flohova
Ondříčkova
Mahlerovy sady
Pospíšilova

Kišťanova
Baranova
Sudoměřská

Palac Floh

knih.
Jagellonská
Bořivojova
Radhošťská

multikino
Cinema City Flora

Ondříčkova Laubova

Jičínská
Ondříčkova

Nejsvětějšího
Srdce Páně
nám.

Přemyslovská
Lucemburská
Orlická
Oličká

Vinohradská
Jiřího z Lobkovic

Jiřího z Poděbrad

Perunova
Slezská
Koněvova
Libická
Blodkova
Čáslavská

Slezská
nám.
Kouřimská
Domažl.
Slavíkov
V Horní
Stromce
střední
fotografická
škola

MŠ
ZŠ

spec.
škola

U Vodárny

Nitranská

Korunní
Korunní
Šrobárova
Šrobárova

Husův sbor
knih.
Řipská
Ruská
Chorvatská
Sobotecká

MŠ
NZ
Dykova

SEVAC
Řicanská
Vlašimská
Bratří Čapků

ZŠ
Benešovská
U Zdravotního ústavu

LV
Hradešínská
MŠ
Bezická
Na Zájezdu
ZA
Ruská

Kotěrova
vila
Na Safránce
Vlašimská

Hradešínská
Na Safránce

Šaliounova
vila
Na Safránce
Ruská

Estonská
Finská
Mexická
Žitomírská
Bulharská

Justiční palác
Konopišťská
28. pluku

Kodaňská
CEU
GYM
ZŠ
Slovenská
28. pluku
Na Míčánkách
Kašťan
Novorossijská

Heroldovy sady
školská
správa
Madridská
Norská

Kodaňská

Ministerstvo životního
prostředí ČR

sv. Mikuláše
spec.
škola
Holandská
sv. Václava
Armenská
Moravská
Chemapol
Archangelská

Vršovické
nám.
Na kovárně
Moskevská
nám.
Svat. Čecha

Kavkazska
Úřad MC
Praha 10
Ruská

Pod Strání
Petrohradská
Orelská
Minská
SŠ
hotelová
úřad práce
Uljanovská
Kozácka

Rostovská
Sportovní
Obloukova
106
Uzbecká

Sámova
T.J.Bohemians
Kodaňská
260
Magnitogorská

Novgorodská
Sportovní
K Louži
Baškírská

F

Petrohradská
LDN
Připotoční
Pod Sychrovem

K Botli
gymnázium
spec. ZŠ pro děti
s vadou řeč.

Hala
Olymp

K Topírně
Vršovický
hřbitov

FÚ P 4
FÚ P 10
hl.
Loupnická
U Seřadiště
K Topírně
Křeslická

Kablovická
150
182
U Seřadiště

Botič
Svahová
Pod Sychrovem
Na Křivce

Jivenská
Napako
Na Sychrově
gymnázium
Na Pátkuu

Mendíků
ZŠ
Čapkova
Magistrů
hl.
Bohdalec
Na Sychrově
Na Bohdalci

Děkanská
Nad Vinným p.
Pod Sychrovem II
Pod Sychrovem I
Modletínská

Pod Strákou
Na Křivce
V Dolině

6
7

STREET INDEX

STREET INDEX